In the Beginning God...

Grades 9 and 10

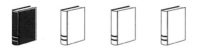

Produced under the auspices of the
North American Division of Seventh-day Adventists
Office of Education

Published by
Pacific Press® Publishing Association
Nampa, Idaho

TABLE OF CONTENTS

WELCOME TO YOUR RELIGION CLASS

This section is intended to provide you with some general information about this textbook and about your religion class.

• THE CROSSROADS SERIES OF RELIGION TEXTBOOKS •

The **CROSSROADS SERIES** is the title of the series of religion textbooks for Seventh-day Adventist secondary schools, grades 9 through 12. This textbook is a part of the series.

The logo for the **CROSSROADS SERIES** symbolizes the theme of the series—that the cross of Jesus Christ is at the very center of Christian faith. God's revelation of Himself in the cross reveals the only sacrifice for sin and the ultimate significance of life to each person and to every nation. Thus the cross stands as the decisive moment of truth for all humankind through all ages. The logo, in symbolic form, portrays the centrality of the cross with all paths(roads) of human experience and personal decisions leading to and from it.

May you meet Jesus at the crossroads of your life and in each decision you make. This is the prayer of those who have prepared these textbooks, and we join our prayer with those of your teacher.

• GOAL OF THE CROSSROADS SERIES •

The goal of the **CROSSROADS SERIES** is that through your study of Scripture in this class you will come to know the loving and redeeming God of Scripture. His self-revelation has its focus and fulfillment in the life, death, resurrection, and intercession of Jesus Christ. His substitutionary death on the cross is the sole basis of Christian assurance. With Christ as Saviour and Lord, each believer is enabled, through the Holy Spirit, to experience a life of worship, growth, and service. Each person is then eager to proclaim and be ready for His return.

• VERSIONS OF THE HOLY BIBLE •

The NEW INTERNATIONAL VERSION, referred to as NIV, is used as the primary version of Scripture for the **Memory Focus**, scriptural references quoted in the narrative section of the lesson, and for answers to **Into the Bible** activities and **Projects**. Other versions of Scripture have also been used when the particular version enriches the meaning of a given reference. Lesson 6 of book 1 will assist you in understanding the difference between a version of the Holy Bible and a translation or a paraphrase.

• REFERENCE BOOKS FOR THE RELIGION CLASS •

Reference books are essential to the religion class. It is important that the following general reference books and books by Ellen G. White are available in your classroom.

1. General Reference books

    a. *The Seventh-day Adventist Bible Commentary*, Vols. 1-8

    b. *The Seventh-day Adventist Bible Dictionary*

    c. *The Seventh-day Adventist Encyclopedia*

    d. A Bible concordance

e. A Bible dictionary

f. A Bible atlas

g. The Seventh-day Adventist Hymnal

h. A current set of encyclopedias

i. A high-school or collegiate dictionary

j. A thesaurus

2. Books by Ellen G. White

a. Conflict of the Ages series
    Patriarchs and Prophets
    Prophets and Kings
    The Desire of Ages
    The Acts of the Apostles
    The Great Controversy

b. *Selected Messages*

c. *Steps to Christ*

d. *Testimonies for the Church*

• MEMORIZATION OF SCRIPTURE •

Each lesson contains a verse labeled **Memory Focus**. Your teacher will assign certain of these verses to be memorized. The references should first be understood, both as to their meaning and to their application to your life. The memorized texts should be reviewed at the end of the lesson and throughout the school year.

• GRADES FOR THE RELIGION CLASS •

Whatever the school policy is regarding grades for the religion class, it is important that you understand your grade is not an evaluation of your spiritual growth or experience. Rather, the grade is an evaluation of the work you do in your religion class and how well you have mastered the content.

Your grade can be based on the following:

1. Class discussion and participation.
2. Your answers to the **Into the Bible** activities.
3. Completion of and/or answers to **Projects**.
4. The results on quizzes and tests.
5. Mastery of the assigned **Memory Focus**.
6. Other criteria identified by your teacher.

CROSSROADS SERIES

unit

1

God's Word and Your Life

Development of the Bible

Unit one focuses on God's Word, the Bible. The lessons will identify the purpose of the Bible as an inspired message from God, its history, the various versions, how it is organized, and how to study it. The introductory lesson (1) focuses on encouraging students to have an inquiring mind.

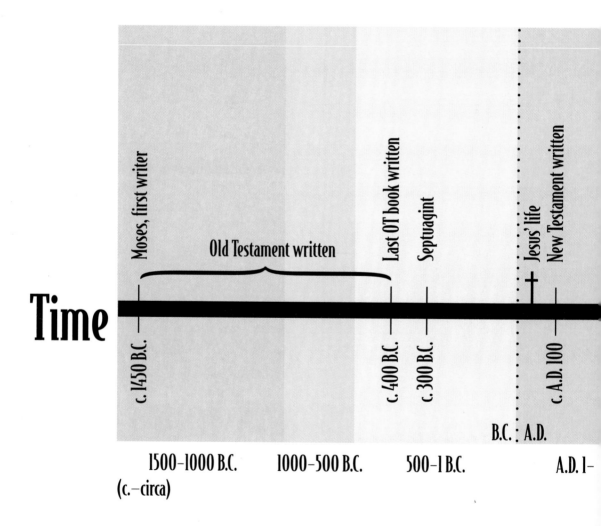

Time

Moses, first writer

Old Testament written

Last OT book written

Septuagint

Jesus' life

New Testament written

c. 1450 B.C.

c. 400 B.C.

c. 300 B.C.

c. A.D. 100

B.C. | A.D.

1500–1000 B.C.   1000–500 B.C.   500–1 B.C.   A.D. 1–

(c.–circa)

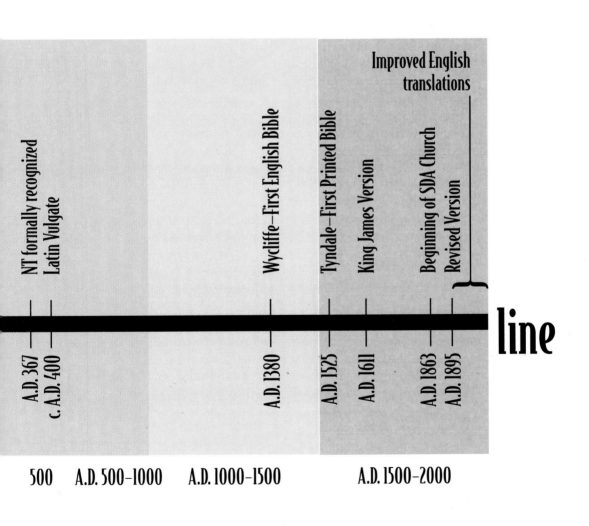

Improved English translations

NT formally recognized — A.D. 367
Latin Vulgate — c. A.D. 400

Wycliffe—First English Bible — A.D. 1380

Tyndale—First Printed Bible — A.D. 1525

King James Version — A.D. 1611

Beginning of SDA Church — A.D. 1863
Revised Version — A.D. 1895

line

500   A.D. 500–1000   A.D. 1000–1500   A.D. 1500–2000

SOLITUDE

The courage to ask must be matched by the wisdom to listen

(Quips and Quotes).

Time Out for Questions

Lesson Scripture: Psalm 73

It's a well-known fact that children ask more questions than adults do. Just ask any parent or teacher of three- or four-year-olds. Kids this age have been "clocked" at as many as thirty questions per hour!

But as we get older, we tend to ask fewer and fewer questions, even about things that truly interest us. Why do we stifle our natural curiosity in this way? There could be many reasons. Some people just naturally keep their thoughts and feelings to themselves. Others are afraid that questions about certain topics will make them appear stupid or ignorant. We've all felt that way at times. When we reach a certain age, we get the idea that there are some topics, like sexuality, that we are supposed to know everything about. So we stop asking questions to avoid feeling inadequate, even though some honest answers and discussion would do us a world of good.

Sometimes we don't ask questions because we're a bit intimidated by the person who would answer them. Not all parents enjoy having their opinions challenged, especially on sensitive subjects like money, politics, or moral values. And debating an issue with one of your teachers can present a whole different set of problems—especially if you must argue in class in front of your fellow students. This is particularly true in the case of your Bible teacher. Somehow we've gotten the idea that Christians shouldn't ask a lot of questions.

13

It implies doubt, distrust, or a negative attitude. But nothing could be farther from the truth.

Honestly searching for answers to questions is positive and constructive. It's the most effective way to learn about anything. And for topics such as relationships, moral values, and religious faith, asking "why" is absolutely essential to understanding and growth. Here's how one student expressed her feelings about curiosity and asking why:

will be opened to you" (Matthew 7:7, TEV). This shows that He understands our need to ask questions. In fact, asking many questions of His religious leaders is one of the few things we know for sure that Jesus did as a boy (Luke 2:46). As a man, Jesus told stories and preached sermons in a way that stimulated questions and challenged people to think for themselves. He never ignored or ridiculed a sincere question.

> I once knew a Man with blood-stained brow
> I wondered why but never asked how
> I heard upon a tree He did die
> But never would I ask Him why.
>
> Today my heart is so unsure
> Could it be that I should have doubted more
> For when my curiosity is high
> I ask, until satisfied, the question "WHY."[1]

---

[1]Hyveth Williams, *Collegiate Quarterly* 9:2, 11.

There is much evidence in the Bible that God expects us to have doubts and will reward our honest questions with truthful answers. Jesus said, "Ask, and you will receive; seek, and you will find; knock, and the door

"Come now, and let us reason together" (Isaiah 1:18, KJV). God makes this offer to everyone, but especially to those who are doubting, discouraged, confused, unbelieving, or just plain angry. He wants to hear our fears and concerns. Jesus invites us, "Come to me, all you who are weary and burdened, and I will give you rest" (Matthew 11:28, NIV). This ought to reassure us that our questions and doubts are welcome.

In this class, you will be encouraged to participate freely in discussions, to express opinions, and to ask questions. So keep in mind that getting useful answers is often a matter of asking questions in the right way. Here are some guidelines that can make class discussions more valuable:

1. Everyone learns more when teachers and students both get a chance to ask and answer questions. Treat other people's questions and opinions with respect. A smirk or sarcastic remark may embarrass a classmate into silence.

2. Don't expect clear, satisfying answers to all your questions. God has promised to supply all our needs, but He hasn't promised to answer all our questions—at least not right away. Some things we will understand better as we get older; others may be a mystery until we get to heaven. Sometimes it's wiser

to say, "I don't know," or, "I don't understand," than to expect solutions to all of life's problems.

3. Be open-minded and sincere. You can be honest without being negative and critical. Some people asked Jesus questions just to trap Him or cause trouble. That approach can be tempting, but it rarely leads to spiritual growth.

4. Asking good, honest questions is only half the struggle. Accepting the right answers is the other half. Whether you're looking for answers to life's basic questions or your own personal problems, you will never regret choosing the Bible as your guide and God as your personal Counselor and Friend. ⭑

 **Memory Focus**

"You will seek Me, and find Me, when you search for Me with all your heart" (Jeremiah 29:13, NKJV).

. . . .

 **Into the Bible**

1. The writer of Psalm 73 asked a lot of searching questions about his trials and disappointments. Read Psalm 73; then respond in writing to the following:

   A. How do you feel about the writer's openness with God?
   B. What is he complaining about?
   C. What did he do to find an answer?
   D. What does he see as the solution?
   E. What can this psalm teach you about dealing with your own frustrations?

. . . .

 Projects

1. This lesson presents four guidelines for personal and classroom Bible study. Can you suggest any others? List them.
2. As you read this lesson, perhaps some of your questions came to mind. Make a list of questions you would like to discuss in class, and give it to your teacher.
3. God welcomes your questions. Make a list of questions you would like to ask God, and discuss them in class.

 **Focus Questions**

1. How can someone overcome the fear of asking questions? How can the teacher help? How can the class help?
2. Jesus said to "ask," "seek," and "knock." How can these things be put into action? Give examples.
3. What are some common excuses people give for not studying the Bible for answers to their questions?
4. This lesson encourages you to express your doubts and concerns, even about spiritual matters. But are there any dangers in doing so? How can we make it less dangerous to express our doubts to others?

17

REVELATION

The cross of Christ reveals God's love at its best and man's sin at its worst
(The Daily Walk).

The Bible: Its Purpose

Lesson Scripture: Luke 24:45, 46

Ever spent any time wondering about the meaning of life? A Jewish map was discovered dating back before the time of Christ. It was a map, all right, but the mapmaker wasn't too interested in the location of empires or countries. He wasn't trying to show people *where* they lived in the world but *how* to understand the world in which they lived.

The map was a series of concentric circles (circles within circles moving inward to the center). The outer circle represented the heavens. Inside that circle was another circle identified as the earth—our planet. At the center of that circle was another circle labeled Judea, the promised land of the Jews. Inside that circle was a circle called Jerusalem, the city of God. Inside that circle was still another circle representing the temple, the house of God. And inside that circle was the final circle, at the very center of the map. It represented the *Most Holy Place*, the dwelling place of God among His people.

CHRIST THE CENTER

That ancient mapmaker was calling his people to center their lives on the presence of God in their midst. The Bible is like his map. Its stories form a series of circles. They move us into the central circle, the *Most Holy Place* of Scripture. That central circle is the life, death, and resurrection of Jesus Christ.

As anyone who has heard a pirate story knows, a good

treasure map always has an *X* marking the spot where the buried gold is found. The Bible is God's treasure map, and the cross is the *X* that points us to salvation through Christ "in whom are hidden **all the treasures** of wisdom and knowledge" (Colossians 2:3, NIV).

THE WORD BECAME FLESH

We call the Bible God's Word. Over 2,000 times in the Old Testament, the prophets declared they were speaking "the word of the Lord" and not just their own words. They repeated to the people what God had spoken to them. Therefore, what they said had authority.

The men who wrote the New Testament claimed even greater authority. They did more than hear the Word of God! They walked with, talked with, and touched the Word of God. His name was Jesus. He who had always been with God—and was God—became a man, and through Him, God drew near to us: "The virgin will be with child and will give birth to a son, and they will call Him 'Immanuel'—which means, 'God with us'" (Matthew 1:23, NIV).

THE STORY OF JESUS FROM GENESIS TO REVELATION

Martin Luther believed the whole Bible pointed to Christ. Luther began his talks with students by reading Psalm 40:7, which says: "In the volume of **the book** it is written of **Me**." Then he would ask two questions:

"What book?"

"The Bible," they would respond.

"And what man?"

"Jesus Christ!"

The Bible is not a loose collection of religious stories. From beginning to end, it is the story of Jesus. It presents all of **history as His story**.

JESUS AS THE LAMB OF GOD FROM GENESIS TO REVELATION

Specifically, the Bible presents Jesus as "the Lamb of God." *At the cross Jesus took upon Himself the sins of the whole world and took them away. That fact is the heart of Scripture.* When John the Baptist first saw Jesus, he said: "Look, the Lamb of God, who takes away the sin of the world" (John 1:29, NIV).

Salvation in Christ is the crimson thread God uses to

weave together the garment of Scripture. Read the following seven references that point to Jesus as the Lamb:

1. In Genesis 3:21, the covering righteousness of <u>the Lamb</u> is *symbolized.*
2. In Genesis 4:1-5, salvation through <u>the Lamb</u> is *dramatized.*
3. In Genesis 22:6-14, God Himself providing <u>the Lamb</u> is *prophesied.*
4. In Exodus 12:21-23, the saving blood of <u>the Lamb</u> is *applied.*
5. In Isaiah 53:4-12, <u>the Lamb</u> is *personified.*
6. In John 1:29, <u>the Lamb</u> is *identified.*
7. In Revelation 5:5-10, the slain but risen <u>Lamb</u> is *glorified.*

WHAT DOES THE BIBLE DO FOR US?

One of the most highly honored films in history, produced in the 1950s, is *Ben Hur: A Tale of the Christ.* Based on the book by the same title, it won eleven Academy Awards. The book's author was General Lew Wallace, who was a lifelong agnostic (someone who doubts the existence of God). General Wallace was especially hostile to Christianity, and after retiring from the military, he determined to write a book exposing all the errors of the Bible.

A close friend agreed to help. They decided to each study the Bible for one year with no communication between them, to independently find all the mistakes and inconsistencies within its pages.

When the year was over, they met. Lew Wallace spoke first about his experience. He had begun the year hostile and sure of his theory that the Bible was a fraud. But as the months went by and his study of the Bible deepened, his hostility grew first to admiration, then to a deep personal faith in the Christ of the Scriptures. Wallace was a Christian! His friend smiled, cleared his throat, and said: "I, too, have become a Christian." The Bible had changed their lives completely.

Because of this experience, Wallace did write a book. But it was the story of a devout Jew's journey to faith in Christ: *Ben Hur: A Tale of the Christ.*

Another man whose life's journey led to an encounter with Christ was the apostle Paul. He wrote to a young man named Timothy, reminding him that "from infancy you have known the holy Scriptures, which are able to make you **wise for salvation through faith in Christ Jesus**" (2 Timothy 3:15, NIV). Trust this wisdom, said Paul, because "all Scripture is God-breathed." In other words, God made sure, through His own inspiration, that the Bible is perfect for its primary purpose of *leading us to salvation through faith in Jesus Christ.* And once Christ is Lord, then "all Scripture is useful for teaching, rebuking, correcting and train-

ing in righteousness" (2 Timothy 3:16, NIV).

Unless we understand the Bible as a book about Jesus Christ, crucified, risen, and returning, it has no real power to save or transform our lives. In fact, it can even be used to hurt us. In Jesus' day, the Jewish Pharisees studied Scripture to prove their own righteousness. Jesus warned them of the results of this approach. He said, "You diligently study the Scriptures because you think that by them you possess eternal life. These are **the Scriptures that testify about me**, and yet you refuse to **come to me** to have life" (John 5:39, 40, NIV).

As we discover Jesus at the center of Scripture, we also find the Bible has real answers for our real questions. God cares about every part of our lives as much as He cares about our eternal salvation. So He made the Bible practical. Its principles teach us how to live and what is important in life.

For instance, rules without a good relationship simply breed rebellion. More than memorizing heavy doctrines, God wants us to really love one another. The Bible concentrates on teaching us to love one another in response to God's great love for us. Jesus invites us to become His friends. There is joy in the journey when you know you're traveling with a friend.

SUMMARY

To know God, to know ourselves, or to know the meaning of life, we need to know Jesus. We need to know personally that He gave us salvation by dying on the cross for our sins and rising again. In that one great event, everything else becomes clear. All the great stories of the Old Testament point toward the life, death, and resurrection of Christ. The entire New Testament points back to it. Writing to new Christians in Corinth, Paul zeroed in on the Bible's most important theme: "For what I received I passed on to you as of first importance: that Christ died for our sins according to the Scriptures, that he was buried, that he was raised on the third day according to the Scriptures" (1 Corinthians 15:3, 4, NIV).

Long ago, a Roman ruler named Pilate asked, "What is truth?" Minutes later, when Jesus came out wearing a crown of thorns and a purple robe, Pilate answered his own question: "Behold the Man." For us to behold this Man Jesus, crucified, risen, and returning, is the goal of Scripture. ⚲

 **Memory Focus**

"Jesus did many other miraculous signs in the presence of his disciples, which are not recorded in this book. But these are written that you may believe that Jesus is the Christ, the Son of God, and that by believing you may have life in his name" (John 20:30, 31, NIV).

 # Into the Bible

1. In your lesson, under the heading, "Jesus As the Lamb of God," seven key passages are listed. Using numbers 3, 4, and 5, complete the chart your teacher will give you to show the parallels between Old Testament symbols and Christ's death and resurrection.

2. The Bible not only teaches the way of salvation through Jesus as our Saviour, but calls us to discipleship with Jesus as Lord. It not only offers us life eternal, but teaches us how to live. Look up the following passages, and identify two specific statements in each one about what it means to follow Jesus as Lord:

   A. Matthew 16:24-26   D. Ephesians 5:1-21
   B. John 15:1-8   E. Ephesians 6:10-18
   C. Matthew 7:21-27

3. The heroes in many stories found in the Old Testament prefigured, or pointed forward, to Jesus. There were striking similarities between their lives and Christ's work for us. The story of Joseph in Genesis 39–47 illustrates this. Jesus, like Joseph, came to His own brothers, but they rejected Him. Like Joseph, He was betrayed, sold for the price of a slave, falsely accused and condemned, but rose up to become ruler of a kingdom. Like Joseph, He provided the bread of life to a starving world and offered forgiveness and a change of clothes to the very ones who betrayed Him.

   Read 1 Samuel 17, the story of David and Goliath. Identify four characteristics or actions of David that you think suggest similarities between David and Jesus in terms of who they were and what they accomplished for their people.

 # Projects

1. Divide into two groups. Group A should read together Luke

24

24:13-32; group B should read together Luke 24:36-49. Each group should select actors, props, and readers to act out, in a skit or pantomime form, the passage it studied. Allow ten minutes to read and discuss the passage; ten minutes to prepare a skit; and several minutes to act it out. When each skit or pantomime is over, identify, as a class, the key themes Jesus was trying to teach His disciples in these post-resurrection Bible studies. List these on the board.

2. Using the passage you selected from Into the Bible 1, draw a picture or write a poem that illustrates the drama of the story found there.

3. The Bible contains principles for living that help us set our priorities for life. Do the following:

   A. Make a list of seven priorities you have for your life.
   B. Read Matthew 22:37-39.
   C. Number your list of priorities in order of importance based on the spiritual principles found in "B."

. . . .

 # Focus Questions

1. Why do you think God gradually revealed Christ as the way of salvation in the Bible instead of just revealing everything at once?

2. Do you think the Old Testament prophets fully understood their predictions of the first coming of Christ?

3. While Christians believe in a personal God whose Word is truth for all people for all time, relativism is the belief that there is no real truth, but only opinion. What difference do these two views of truth make in daily life?

4. Why do rules without relationship tend to breed rebellion?

5. How could the Pharisees study the Bible so much and be so hardhearted and wrong about who God is?

PRAYER

I will answer them before they even call to me. While they are still talking to me about their needs, I will answer their prayers (Isaiah 65:24, TLB).

lesson 3

The Bible: Its Inspiration

Lesson Scriptures: Genesis 3; Exodus 19; Luke 23

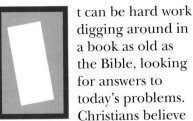t can be hard work digging around in a book as old as the Bible, looking for answers to today's problems. Christians believe the Bible is God's special message to human beings, but sometimes we wonder: Couldn't God have come up with a better way of communicating with us?

To answer that question, we'll consider various ways of communicating. Then we'll take a closer look at the Bible itself as an inspired message from God. But first, the easy part: What is the purpose of God's inspired message? Jesus declared that everything in Scripture can be summarized in two great commands—love to God and love for each other (Matthew 22:35-40). The goal is always to help us love God wholeheartedly and care more deeply for His creation in ways that are in harmony with God's will.

Now let's look at why God chose a book to get the word out.

QUESTION 1

WHY WON'T GOD ANSWER HIS PHONE?

God's problem communicating with sinful creatures

Today, if you want to send a message to someone, you have lots of choices:

a. Visit in person.
b. Call on the phone.
c. Send a video.
d. Write a letter.
e. Ask another person to go and take the message for you.
f. Ask a good writer to send a

27

message for you.

g. Send flowers, chocolates, or something else nice.

Which option would you choose? Would you always choose the same method?

Imagine that someone very important wants to send a message to you. Suppose the President, the prime minister, the governor, or maybe the General Conference president has some good news for you personally. How would they get the message to you? How would you like to receive such significant news?

Now imagine something a little more realistic. Suppose that after your last class of the day, your teacher slips you a note that reads, "Go see the principal immediately in her office," or worse yet, "Go immediately to the principal's office. A police officer is waiting to see you." What would be your first reaction?

If you knew you had been acting up lately—skipping classes, throwing rocks through store windows—you would probably expect the worst. You would hardly imagine that the principal wanted to ask how she could help or that the police

just wanted to encourage you to get an after-school job.

Even if you were a model student and citizen, would your first thought be that you had won a scholarship? or that the police department wanted to honor you as an outstanding student? When people in authority say they have a message for us, most of us automatically feel a little chill up the spine, and an inner voice says, "Uh-oh."

Knowing this about people, what would you do if you were the school principal or the police officer? Whether you had good news or bad, what would be the best way to deliver your message without frightening someone to death? Would it be best to ring their doorbell unannounced? Call them at home? Send a note?

Now bring God into this picture. He always wants to get through to you; you sometimes want to get through to Him. He always has an important message for you; you don't always want to hear from Him. How should God get through to you? In a sinless world, it wouldn't matter. You wouldn't be afraid to hear from God at any time. But knowing what you know

28

about yourself, would you really want God to ring your doorbell unannounced?

Just to complicate matters further, sometimes you really do want to get through to God. You send an urgent "call," but it seems His line is busy or out of order. You wish that you had a hotline to God and that He would always answer your calls. But wait. What if the hotline were a two-way connection? Of course you want God to pick up whenever you call Him. But what if He could call you whenever you seemed to be getting out of line? Have you ever worked for a boss who didn't trust you, who was always looking over your shoulder offering advice and criticism? It wasn't much fun, was it? Imagine a God who pounced on your every move like that!

Let's face it. God on our doorstep, or even at the other end of a hotline, is just too scary. God knows that. That's why He asked special messengers to write about Him and put it all in a book in words we can understand and receive as we are ready. After all, God doesn't want to frighten us; He wants to communicate with us.

 # Into the Bible

1. God finally "answers the phone."

The three texts listed below tell three very different stories about God's attempts to communicate with frightened and guilty human beings. Read and compare these three stories, and imagine yourself as one of the participants.

- God comes walking in the garden: Genesis 3:8-24
- God thunders from a smoking mountain: Exodus 19:16-25
- God comes to die on a cross: Luke 23:32-40

A. For each of the three references, write down how you would have felt about God's approach to humans if you had been there yourself. Is there anything about these stories that makes you love God more? Explain.

B. List two advantages of reading or hearing these stories from a book, rather than experiencing them firsthand.

QUESTION 2

WHAT KIND OF TEACHER COMMUNICATES BEST?

*Blending the human and the divine
to get the message through*

Fred's parents wanted him to learn to play the piano. Fred wasn't very enthusiastic, but he reluctantly went along with the plan.

His first teacher was Mrs. J. She was hard and seemed mean, even though she probably didn't intend to be. Sometimes Fred was upset when he got home from his piano lesson. He learned a lot. But it wasn't much fun.

When Fred's dad changed jobs, the family had to move, and Fred got a new piano teacher—Mrs. K. She really was nice. No matter how well or badly Fred played, Mrs. K. always said nice things. He liked Mrs. K. a lot. But he couldn't understand why he didn't learn very much. After a while, practicing was even less fun than it was for Mrs. J.

Another move, another teacher. Mr. L. could play better than anyone Fred had ever heard. But when Fred played for him, Mr. L. got very impatient, even angry. "No, no!" he would shout. "Here. Let me show you how." Embarrassed but amazed,

Fred would watch and listen. The piano sounded so exciting when Mr. L. played, but Fred knew he could never play that way. He wasn't sure he even wanted to try.

Fred eventually learned to play the piano quite well. He even ended up being a piano teacher himself. Over the years, he thought a lot about what he learned and did not learn from Mrs. J., Mrs. K., and Mr. L.

From what kind of teacher do you learn best? In music? In sports? In history? In English? In math? What kind of teacher is most effective in helping you learn about God?

Even in your class, not all the students will be able to learn equally well from every teacher. Some teachers are very bright and quick; others are more methodical. Some are friendly and warm; others are distant and businesslike. Some don't teach very well even though they are well-trained; some are excellent teachers even though they have had little formal training. Generally, we learn best from teachers who understand us and know how to communicate well.

In that regard, see what Ellen White has to say about the value of having different

teachers teach us about God: "In our schools the work of teaching the Scriptures to the youth is not to be left wholly with one teacher for a long series of years. . . . Different teachers should have a part in the work, even though they may not all have so full an understanding of the Scriptures."[1]

Given all the different kinds of people in the world, God needs many different messengers to reach them all.

 # Into the Bible

2. Finding the Best Teacher

Let's look at three writing techniques and see how God can use them to make His Word more effective.

A. Using Various Sources. Sometimes we assume the writers of Scripture got all their words from God in visions. But the Spirit also directed God's messengers to use human sources to augment their divine visions and guided them in the conclusions they reached. In general, there are three sources of an inspired message, as listed below. Consider them carefully; then complete the exercise that follows.

(1) Direct revelation
(2) Research in various written sources
(3) Personal observation, experience, or conversations with people

Matching: Read each of the following passages, and indicate the source of the message using the above three categories.

_____ Author of Chronicles: The life of Jehoshaphat, found in 2 Chronicles 20:31-34.
_____ Balaam: The blessings, found in Numbers 23.
_____ Solomon: The wise counsel, found in Proverbs 10.
_____ Paul: The divisions in the church at Corinth, found in 1 Corinthians 1:10-17.

[1] White, Ellen G. *Counsels to Parents, Teachers, and Students,* (Boise, ID: Pacific Press Publishing Assn., 1943), 432.

Into the Bible (continued)

Even though some sources may seem more human than divine, the Spirit still molded them into a unified, inspired message. "All Scripture is inspired by God" (2 Timothy 3:16, NRSV), regardless of its source.

    B. Adapting a Message to Particular Needs. Under the guidance of the Spirit, God's messengers could choose to be gentle or firm, depending on what their listeners or readers needed to hear. Compare the following passages:

        (1) Attitudes toward the Sabbath: Compare Nehemiah 13:15-22 and Matthew 12:1-14. Which text suggests that God's people had become careless in keeping the Sabbath? Which one indicates that they had become too rigid? Which of the two stories applies to our needs today? Can you think of possible instances where either story might be applied?

        (2) Attitudes toward divorce: Compare Nehemiah 13:23-27 and Matthew 19:1-12. Which biblical account would be most helpful in the church today? Why?

The school board hired your principal but did not spell out every detail of how to run the school. Your principal hires teachers but doesn't tell them exactly what to say and do in the classroom. It's the same with inspired writers. God sometimes gives precise instructions, but generally, the Spirit guides God's messengers to consider the needs of the people and speak accordingly.

    C. "Coloring" the Message With the Writer's Temperament and Personality. Paul is one of the more volatile writers in Scripture. Compare the general tone of 1 Corinthians 5 with 1 Corinthians 13. Why is one message so hard and the other so soft? Do you know people who can switch personal styles like that? Do you think God needs to be hard or soft with you? What color would you use to capture the tone for each passage?

QUESTION 3
HOW DO I KNOW THE BIBLE IS FROM GOD?
Trust the Book.

Some devoted Christians try to prove *that the Bible is true.* They often use arguments from science or archæology to make their points. Some of these arguments can be very helpful, but they cannot prove that the Bible is from God.

Another group of people, many of them angry with God or religion, try to prove that the Bible is not true. They, too, use arguments from science or archæology to make their points. But they cannot disprove the truth of the Bible any more than believers can prove it.

God doesn't leave us without evidence for faith, but ultimately we have to trust Him just as we trust our friends. If we tried to prove in some absolute way that our friends are true friends, we would drive them away, for trying to prove trust actually destroys it.

A much more powerful argument for the truth of the Bible is found in the experience of the Christian. Ellen White puts it this way:

"In its power, men and women have broken the chains of sinful habit. They have renounced selfishness. The profane have become reverent, the drunken sober, the profligate pure. Souls that have borne the likeness of Satan have been transformed into the image of God. This change is itself the miracle of miracles. A change wrought by the word, it is one of the deepest mysteries of the word. We cannot understand it; we can only believe, as declared by the Scriptures, it is 'Christ in you, the hope of glory.' Colossians 1:27" (*Education*, 172). ⚐

3 3

Memory Focus

"All scripture is inspired by God and is useful for teaching, for reproof, for correction, and for training in righteousness, so that everyone who belongs to God may be proficient, equipped for every good work" (2 Timothy 3:16, 17, NRSV).

Projects

1. **Different Ways of Hearing God's Message.** Even though we may not have visions or hear God's voice directly, from the Bible we can learn about other people's experiences with God. Select one or more of the texts listed below, and ask yourself the following questions: What does this passage teach me about God? Does the form of the message (story, song, prayer, sermon) make it harder or easier to understand?

   A. A Prayer of Sadness: Psalm 22.
   B. A Song of Joy: Psalm 100.
   C. A Story of a Dream: Nebuchadnezzar's Image: Daniel 2.
   D. A Prophet's Message of Warning: Amos 4.
   E. A Story of a Prophet's Birth: 1 Samuel 1:1-18.

2. **The Bible's Effect on Your Life.**

   A. Think about how the Bible has affected your life, the lives of your friends, or people you have known or heard about. Has the Bible always been helpful, or has it sometimes made it more difficult to believe in God and trust His goodness?
   B. Think about stories in the Bible that seem to make it harder to believe that God loves us. Do you know someone who claims they no longer believe in God because of a particular Bible story? Write down two of these difficult stories; choose

one, and read it again. Search for good answers. Is there anything in the life and teachings of Jesus that might make the story easier to understand? Compare notes with your classmates. Ask your parents or your teacher for help.

C. Write down some of the good ways the Bible has influenced your life. Share this list with your classmates.

· ·

 Focus Questions

1. What would be the advantages and disadvantages of God's speaking to us directly more often?
2. Can you think of any benefits of having stories in the Bible that we don't like?
3. Which of these is the biggest obstacle to your finding more help from the Bible: It is too: (a) violent; (b) discouraging; (c) boring; (d) hard to understand? Can you think of good "solutions" to these problems?
4. Can you think of part of the Bible that is helpful to you but is hurtful to someone else? Do you know of parts of the Bible that are a problem for you but actually are helpful to someone else?
5. How do you know when to trust a message from someone in your life? Does trust in the Bible come in the same way?
6. What are some stories in the Bible you dislike? Why? Why do you think they were put in the Bible?

WISDOM

If any of you lacks wisdom, he should ask God, who gives generously to all without finding fault, and it will be given to him (James 1:5, NIV).

The Bible: Its Construction

Lesson Scripture: 1 Peter 1:10-12

LOOKING INSIDE THE ARK

Is there anything you can touch that is as sacred or holy as the Bible? What about a hymnal or the church pulpit? Maybe the juice and bread at the Lord's Supper?

These may be the holiest objects you can think of today, but they really can't compare to the tabernacle God commanded Moses to build in the desert. No modern church could have the same feeling of holiness as that tent with its sacred court, its Holy Place, and finally the Most Holy Place with the ark containing the Ten Commandments written by God's own finger.

At your church, the Sabbath School rooms probably aren't as special as the main sanctuary, which isn't quite as special as the pulpit. When you were little, the pastor, a deacon, or your parents might have scolded you if you ran around the church on Sabbath or played hide-and-seek behind the pulpit.

Can you imagine running around and playing games in the Most Holy Place of Moses' tabernacle? The Bible tells of people who dropped dead just for touching the ark of the covenant (1 Samuel 4–6 and 2 Samuel 6). It's hard to imagine anything holier than the tabernacle and the ark.

Do you think of your Bible as being that holy? Maybe it's in your locker right now, along with your math, history, and science books. Perhaps you were taught to make sure nothing rested on top of the Bible and to handle it with great respect, as though it were very holy.

That's not such a bad idea, really. The strange thing is that many people find their attitude toward the Bible changes the more they seriously attempt to understand its message. As they try to apply biblical teachings to their own lives, the Bible gradually seems less like a holy, sacred object they are fearful to touch, and more like a letter from a good friend—a letter they can hardly wait to open. Maybe that's what Jesus had in mind when He told His disciples they were no longer His servants, but His friends (John 15:15).

As you begin to see the Bible as something less mysterious and more practical, you may find your attitude changing too—and it may make you a bit uneasy. You may feel as though the Bible as a book is less holy, even as the God revealed in it is becoming more awesome and holy in your life. Through faith in Christ, the Bible becomes a letter from a friend—and more precious than ever before.

And that's what God wants. Pick up the Bible, read it, ponder it, understand it. These are things you can do for yourself. You don't have to rely on the teacher or preacher. In her day, Ellen White worried that ordinary people would leave Bible study to the experts. "We are not to accept the opinion of commentators as the voice of God; they are erring mortals like ourselves. God has given reasoning powers to us as well as them" *(Testimonies to Ministers,* 106).

The Old Testament describes people standing back from the holy mountain, from the holy sanctuary, from the holy ark. But when Jesus came, people saw holiness in a new light. Jesus taught that He Himself would now be the bridge between God and His people. That excited John. He watched Jesus heal and give hope to desperate lives. He saw Jesus triumph on the cross. Later he wrote the early Christians about a real Messiah who lived a real life; whose blood cleansed us from all our sins. That's why John and the other disciples called the word about Jesus "gospel," which means good news. Today, the good news about Jesus comes to us in a book we call the Bible. Just as John saw and touched Jesus, we can see Him and experience His touch through

the Bible. We can learn how God led devout people to cherish His word and put it in writing so that we can have copies in our lockers, on our desks, beside our beds. We are God's friends, and the Bible is His letter to us.

HOW THE BIBLE IS ORGANIZED

The Bible used by Protestant Christians is divided into two parts: the Old and New Testaments. The word *testament* isn't used much today. Basically, it means an agreement, or promise, between two people or groups. In this instance, it means a promise from God to His people.

Old Testament. The old promise is simply the one that God gave first. In fact, this part of our Bible was the whole Bible used by Jesus and the apostles. It contains the history, laws, and poetry of God's people from creation to shortly before the time of Christ. In English Bibles, the 39 books of the *Old Testament* are organized into groups according to their content style (though many of the books contain elements of more than one group). Within each group, the books are roughly chronological:

➤ **Law:**
  Genesis to Deuteronomy
  (5 books)
➤ **History:**
  Joshua to Esther
  (12 books)
➤ **Poetry:**
  Job to Song of Solomon
  (5 books)
➤ **Prophecy:**
  Isaiah to Malachi
  (17 books)

New Testament. In the years immediately following Jesus' ascension, the disciples used

what we call the Old Testament as their Bible and simply told the people how Jesus fulfilled these earlier promises, or testaments. Most scholars agree that the first book of what we now call the New Testament was Paul's first letter, or "epistle," to the church at Thessalonica, probably written about fifteen years after Jesus' ascension. Of the four Gospels, the first written was probably done by Mark some thirty years after the end of Jesus' earthly ministry. Up to that time, stories about Jesus had been told by eyewitnesses and passed on by word of mouth, or in sermons.

In time, it became clear that this "new covenant" community needed a more permanent record of what God had done for them through Jesus. So the written stories about Jesus (gospels), the acts of the early church leaders (history), the letters to believers (epistles), and John's vision of the triumph of God's kingdom (apocalypse) were brought together to form the New Testament. Lists of these books began to circulate. The first formal list of the complete New Testament as we know it appeared in AD 367. Athanasius, bishop of Alexan-

dria, Egypt, sent an Easter letter to the churches in his jurisdiction, listing for the first time the twenty-seven books that make up our *New Testament.*

The process by which these books came together is called "canonization," a topic we will come to later. For now, let's see how the New Testament is divided into groups:

➢ **Gospels:**
   Matthew to John
   (4 books)
➢ **History:**
   Acts of the Apostles
   (1 book)
➢ **Epistles:**
   Romans to Jude
   (21 books)
➢ **Apocalypse:**
   Revelation
   (1 book)

In the next section we discover what the Bible itself tells us about how the books of the Bible were written.

WRITERS OF THE BIBLE

The authors of the sixty-six books of the Bible wrote to God's people on God's behalf about immediate needs and circumstances. But beyond this, they sensed they were pointing to something so much greater— God's saving work through Jesus Christ.

Many of the books of the New Testament come with an author's name attached. But scholars are not sure who wrote most of the Old Testament.

Even if we don't know the authors' names, many of the books of the Bible do tell us something about how they were written. Let's look more closely at what the Bible itself says about the writing of its individual books.

 # Into the Bible

1. **New Testament Books.** Read the following verses to discover what they say about how a gospel or epistle is written:

   A. Luke 1:1-4
   B. Romans 16:22
   C. 1 Corinthians 16:21
   D. Galatians 6:11

   From these verses, you may have discovered that the biblical writers didn't do all the work themselves, or receive all their ideas in visions. Sometimes, like Luke, they did research. Paul employed secretaries to help him write his letters.

2. **Old Testament Books.** Study the following passages, and identify how various people worked together to produce a book of the Bible.

   A. Proverbs 25:1; 30:1; 31:1
   B. Jeremiah 36; 51:59-64
   C. Deuteronomy 34

   These verses reveal that even books with an author's name may not have been written entirely by that person. Many of the proverbs were written by Solomon, but some are the work of others. Hezekiah lived around 200 years after the time of Solomon. His people collected and compiled the proverbs of Solomon.

Into the Bible (continued)

Jeremiah had help writing his book. Someone who cherished Jeremiah's words added the last chapter to his book after the prophet's death, to show how Jeremiah's prophecies were fulfilled. This may have been done by Baruch, Jeremiah's secretary.

Finally, Deuteronomy, the last book written by Moses, describes his death and burial, something he could not have written himself. One Jewish tradition says that Moses saw his own death in a vision and put it in writing before he died. It is more likely, however, that an associate of Moses, possibly Joshua, wrote chapter 34 of Deuteronomy, which adds a note about Moses' death.

MAKING THE BIBLE EASIER TO READ
Chapters, Paragraphs, Verses

Besides not being in its original language, your Bible differs from early versions in many ways. For instance, ancient Bibles were not divided into chapters and verses. In fact, some New Testament manuscripts didn't even separate words from each other.

Alltheletterssimplyrantogeth erinonecontinuouswordorso itwouldappear.

And if you think that sentence is hard to read in your own language, try one like it in a foreign one!

In some early manuscripts, paragraphs and sections were marked. But chapters and verses didn't become common until the Reformation. One interesting legend credits the verse divisions in the New Testament to Robert Stephanus, an early printer of the Bible. As the story goes, he made the divisions while riding horseback between Paris and Lyons, France, the occasional bad divisions being the fault of the horse.

All modern English translations of the Bible are divided into chapters; most have verses and paragraphs as well. Some eliminate the verse numbers because they detract from reading continuously (Phillip's New Testament and the Reader's Digest

Bible, for example). See Project 2, if you want to explore the readability of different versions of the Bible.

SUMMARY

Similar to the way God came into a very human world in the form of His Son, Jesus, so He has sent His word by means of human messengers. And these messengers sometimes had human helpers as well. So we come back to the question we started with: Is your Bible any different from your other books?

We could answer with a comparison. In some ways, the wood and gold that comprised the ark of the covenant were just like the wood and gold everywhere else in the world. But when God guided His people to form that wood and gold into a sacred vessel for His Ten Commandments, it became very special indeed. It became holy, not to be carelessly handled or looked into.

Our Bible is made of paper, ink, and words, just like other books. But when the paper, ink, and words are uniquely used by the Holy Spirit to make the Bible, they become sacred and holy. In some ways, it is dangerous to look into that sacred book carelessly. But if we reverently search for Jesus through its pages, it will not destroy, but give life and salvation. That's why it's such a special Book. Open it, read it, ponder it. Accept the salvation it freely offers, and obey the Lord it proclaims. ⚐

Memory Focus

"Above all, you must understand that no prophecy of Scripture came about by the prophet's own interpretation. For prophecy never had its origin in the will of man, but men spoke from God as they were carried along by the Holy Spirit" (2 Peter 1:20, 21, NIV).

OR

The books of the Bible in order.

Into the Bible

3. Reverence For the Holy. Read Revelation 1:3 and 22:17, 18 and describe what these verses teach about the attitude we should have toward Scripture.
4. The Bible Jesus Used. In Luke 11:51, Jesus referred to the murder of Abel and Zechariah. These stories are told in Genesis 4:1-16 and 2 Chronicles 24:15-22. Chronicles is the last book of the Hebrew Bible and Zechariah's murder is the last recorded death of a prophet in Chronicles. Read these two passages along with Luke 11:37-54. Can you explain why Jesus would refer to these two incidents?

Projects

1. **Books of the Bible in Rhythm.** Learn to recite the books of the Bible in order and in rhythm. Work with members of your class to develop a rhythmic pattern everyone can learn to say aloud, in unison.

2. **Finding a Readable Bible.** Select a specific passage of the Bible, such as a story from the gospels or the Old Testament, and read it in several different translations. Note how the placement of the verses, paragraphs, and chapters makes it easier or harder to read. Start with the King James Version, where the paragraph divisions are hard to spot, and compare the passage with several other modern Bibles.

. . . .

 # Focus Questions

1. How do you feel about the Bible? Is it like a letter from a very important person, or a letter from your very best friend? Is it like both of these things?
2. What makes a book holy? What makes anything holy? Was holiness more common in Bible times than it is today?
3. How important is it to arrive at the right interpretation of the Bible? How can you be sure your interpretation is right? Is it dangerous to rely on what your pastor or teacher says is right?
4. Which parts of the Bible are most interesting to read? Most difficult? Why are the difficult parts included in the Bible?
5. Author, secretary, copyist, translator, reader. For whom is the work of the Holy Spirit most important? Least important? Put this list in order of importance and explain your choices.

DIRECTION

The Ten Commandments are not multiple choice (Unknown).

The Bible: Its History

Lesson Scriptures: Hebrews 1:1, 2; I Peter 1:10-12

CANON: PUTTING THE BOOKS OF THE BIBLE TOGETHER TO STAY

Who would be the most likely person you know to have a vision from God?

Now imagine that this person wrote out the vision. How would you know if it was inspired; equal to the Bible?

God told Israel that when there were prophets among them, "I the LORD make myself known to them in visions; I speak to them in dreams" (Numbers 12:6, NRSV).

Everyone has ordinary dreams. But the prophets knew when a special vision came from God. In New Testament times, the gift of prophecy especially focused on "the testimony of Jesus." In that light, Ephesians 4:11-13 records God's promise that the various gifts of the Spirit would be found among God's people until the full unity of the faith is reached. Among the gifted ones would be prophets, evangelists, pastors, and teachers.

Adventists believe the gifts will continue until Jesus' second coming. The promise of a continued prophetic gift is part of the reason why Adventists accept that God could speak through Ellen White in dreams and visions.

The question of what belongs in our Bible is a question of canon. Originally (in Greek), the word *canon* referred to a straight reed that could be used as a kind of measuring rod or standard. In our modern religious world, the word *canon* refers to a specific collection of sacred writings that provide a measuring rod or standard for a particular religious community. Often differences in canon serve to mark off the boundaries of a group of believers. Note how each of the following religious groups accepts a different canon:

➤ Islam: The Koran

➤ Samaritans: First five books of Moses (the Law)

➤ Judaism: Hebrew Bible (Old Testament: Law, Prophets, Writings)

➤ Protestants: Old Testament and New Testament

➤ Roman Catholics: Old Testament, New Testament, Apocrypha

➤ Latter-day Saints (Mormons): Old Testament, New Testament, Book of Mormon, and two other books.

In one way or another, all the above groups trace their roots back to Abraham. Mormonism is the most recent movement and adds modern writings to an otherwise Protestant canon. In a sense, Islam is also a more recent development, originating with the prophet Mohammed some six hundred years after the time of Christ. Even though it has its own distinct sacred writings, the Koran, Islam still traces its roots back to Abraham through Ishmael.

With the exception of Islam, all the above groups share at least one group of writings in common, the books of Moses. The Samaritans have the smallest canon, since they accept only the books of Moses. The Jewish Bible includes all that the Samaritans accept plus the Prophets and Writings. Protestants accept all that the Jews accept but add the New Testament. The Catholic Bible includes all that the Jews and Protestants accept plus the Apocrypha. Mormons accept the Protestant Bible plus three additional books of their own.

For the communities with Jewish-Christian roots, major controversies and significant historical events played important roles in their decisions of what should be viewed as Scripture. The most significant events are worth knowing.

The Old Testament: The Samaritan Schism

An important event for both Jews and Samaritans is described in 2 Kings 17. Assyria conquered the northern kingdom of Israel

(722 B.C.). Many Jews were taken into exile, and the Assyrians replaced them with conquered peoples from elsewhere. These people, known as Samaritans, were of mixed blood and mixed religion.

In 587/586 B.C., Babylonians conquered the rest of the tribes of Jacob, the ones in the southern kingdom of Judah. They destroyed Jerusalem and its temple in the process. Nebuchadnezzar had already taken a number of Jews captive to Babylon, including Daniel and his companions in 605 B.C. and the prophet Ezekiel in 597 B.C.

In 536 B.C., some of the exiles came back to Judah from Babylon. One of their first tasks was to rebuild the temple. Their half-relatives, the Samaritans, offered to help. But the Jews wouldn't let them.

In time, the tensions between the Jews and Samaritans led to almost complete separation between the two groups. When the separation came between Jews and Samaritans, the Samaritans took with them the only part of the Hebrew Bible that had attained true canonical status at that point in history, the Law of Moses: Genesis, Exodus, Leviticus, Numbers, and Deuteronomy.

Although God's people had cherished the books of Moses for centuries, the Samaritan schism was an important visible event in the development of the Jewish-Christian canon. It was now clear that the Law of Moses had become the "Bible" in the fullest sense.

By the time of Jesus, the other two parts of the Hebrew Bible, Writings and Prophets, had also become canon in the fullest sense. But almost no evidence remains that would help us understand just how these additional books became part of our Old Testament.

Luke 24:44 suggests that the Old Testament as we know it was complete in Jesus' day, for on the Emmaus road, He mentions all three parts of the Hebrew Bible: Law, Prophets, and Psalms (the largest book in the Writings).

The New Testament: Christianity separates from Judaism

The New Testament makes it clear that the Hebrew Bible was the Bible of Jesus and His apostles. They preached from it, argued from it, quoted from it. The New Testament writers, however, were not using the Hebrew language, but Greek. Understandably, then, when

they quoted from the Old Testament, they usually did so from a Greek translation, usually the widely known Septuagint (LXX).

The New Testament also makes clear that not all Jews were convinced that Jesus was the Jewish Messiah. Jesus Himself was a Jew; His disciples were Jews and preached in Jewish synagogues; indeed, much of early Christian missionary work was among Jews. But Christianity remained a minority movement within Judaism.

As the main body of Jews continued to resist the Christian message, the apostles increasingly turned their attention to the Gentiles. Eventually, the gulf between Jews and Christians became so wide that Christians almost seemed to forget that Jesus was a Jew and had used the Jewish Bible.

As the apostles spoke and wrote about Jesus, their words started a new collection of books that eventually would be known as the New Testament. Gospels and epistles would make up the greater part of the New Testament, plus one book of history (Acts) and one book of apocalypse (Revelation).

We know of no books written by Jesus Himself. His words and sayings, along with stories of His life and miracles, were passed on by those who first heard them from Jesus. People collected those stories and sayings to pass on to others. About thirty years after Jesus' ascension, the first book was written.

Luke, in the introduction to his Gospel, hints at what was beginning to happen. So many people were telling stories about Jesus that some of them weren't getting it right (see Luke 1:1-4). So he went back to those who knew Jesus personally to get the story right. Matthew and John were themselves apostles, and Mark was Peter's penman. Eventually, their Gospels became part of our Bible: Matthew, Mark, Luke, and John. Other gospels were written by other people, but they did not bear the marks of inspiration or authenticity and were not included in the Bible.

Something similar happened to the epistles. Not even a letter written by an apostle automatically became part of the Bible. A careful reading of Paul's letters to the church at Corinth indicates that he sent them more than two letters. We don't know what happened to the other letters. Our Bible includes only two.

Again, in the course of time, so many letters were circulating among the early Christians that it became difficult to determine which ones were genuine and faithful to the story of Jesus. Typically, if it could be known that one of the apostles had written a letter, then it was cherished and preserved. Lists of genuine letters were drawn up by church leaders so that Christians might know which letters had been accepted by other churches.

In A.D. 367, the Christian bishop of Alexandria, in Egypt, sent out an "Easter Letter" to the area churches in which he listed the twenty-seven New Testament books. That is the first complete list on record that includes just the twenty-seven, no more and no less. Issues surrounding the New Testament canon were finally settled some three hundred years after Jesus had given His gospel commission to His disciples.

The Apocrypha: Demoted by Protestants, Promoted by Catholics

The books labeled "Apocrypha" were all written by Jews in the period between the Testaments. Many resemble books in our Old Testament. First and Second Maccabees, for example, are historical books like Kings and Chronicles. Ecclesiasticus is a wisdom book like Proverbs.

As the Apocrypha circulated among Christians, they were sometimes viewed almost as Scripture, sometimes simply as devotional literature. As the centuries passed, the apocryphal books came more and more to be seen as only devotional, not part of the authentic canon. In the sixteenth century, Protestant Reformers insisted that all church teachings must have a biblical basis. Since Catholic teachings such as purgatory could only be defended from apocryphal books, the Catholic Council of Trent (1546) declared the Apocrypha to be Scripture, as the Old and New Testaments are. Something of a final step in the Protestant demotion of the Apocrypha came in 1827 when the British and American Bible Societies decided that they would no longer include the Apocrypha in their published translations of the Bible.

Canonization: Summary

In one sense, canonization (the approval of a collection of

writings that serves as an authoritative standard) could simply be viewed as a human process in much the same way as the writing of an epistle or a psalm could be seen as merely a human activity. But for those who have a Christian view of the canon, three key points are worth emphasizing.

1. God was as much involved in the formation of the canon as He was in inspiring the prophetic messages in the first place. Christians firmly accept both GOD'S INSPIRING and GUIDING role in the creation of the Bible, even when the process seems to have involved quite ordinary people in the church.

2. The process of canonization was not simply brought about by an official decree of the Christian church, although at times that did occur. Over a lengthy period of time, it involved the shared judgment of the entire community of believers, guided by the Holy Spirit, to COLLECTIVELY RECOGNIZE AND ACCEPT as canon those books that the Holy Spirit had originally inspired through individual writers. From the time the message was first written,

while it was being read, studied, and applied, until it was compiled, collected, and officially confirmed as canon, God clearly emerges as the Chief Architect of His Word.

3. Whenever the body of Christian believers made a decision about holy writings being recognized as canon, any new addition had to measure up to the following criteria: the NEW HAD TO AGREE WITH THE OLD—the already established books of Scripture. "To the Law and to the Testimony, if they speak not according to this word it is because there is no light in them" (Isaiah 8:20, KJV). Along with this, the writer had to qualify as a duly recognized prophet, apostle, or inspired eyewitness. And as concluding evidence, the message had to have the confirming witness of the Holy Spirit.

II. THE BIBLE IN ENGLISH

Toss out the TV and VCR, the radio, and all your books, magazines, and newspapers. There's nothing left in the house to read. Nothing. Furthermore, you've forgotten how to read. No, it's worse than that.

Into the Bible

1. Bible or not? Can you tell? Listed below are several popular sayings. Which ones are from the Bible? Which one is not in the Protestant Bible? Read Proverbs 11:24, 25; 15:1; 17:22.

A cheerful heart is good medicine.
A penny saved is a penny earned.
A soft answer deflects wrath.
The more some give, the more they gain.

The Bible faithfully reveals how God has worked with the human family. Yet many good and true things have been spoken and written that are not found in the Bible. Such good things are measured by the Bible, for Christians insist that it is the standard by which we judge all else. That's what *canon* means: "rule" or "standard."

Unless a person is thoroughly familiar with all the Bible, it would be hard even for a very devout Christian to select from a pile of stories and sayings the exact ones that belong to the Bible. The larger Christian community, under the guidance of the Spirit, has played an important role in preserving the canon for us.

You never knew how to read.

Now you're close to the way it was in England in A.D. 596 when Augustine of Canterbury, a Roman Catholic missionary, came to the British Isles. Christians, known as the Celtic church, were already present when Augustine came. Gradually, they were brought under Catholic control. But whether Celtic or Catholic, ordinary people couldn't read. So, as an ordinary person, what would you do with a Bible? Not much.

In later times, missionaries would have set up a school so that you could learn to read. This would make it possible for you to have your own Bible and read it for yourself. But when Augustine first came to English-speaking lands, schools weren't popular, and for good reason—the official medieval church (Catholic) held firmly to two deeply rooted convictions:

A. The Word of God could be given in Latin only (those

ancient English people knew about as much Latin as you do!).

B. Common people were not permitted to learn to read Latin, or any other language, for that matter, certainly not English.

The priests and monks would tell the people what they should know and do. The church leaders sensed that it would be dangerous to let ordinary people read the Bible for themselves. They might start asking questions. Who knew what would happen if people asked questions?

But the people were hungry for the Word of God. Somehow, they had to find a way to hear it in words they could understand. Let's look at the steps that gradually brought the Bible into the hands of the people in their own language.

1. **Poetry: A.D. 600.** First, the people began to make poetry. They would sing and remember and sing again. They made dramas and performed them. One of the earliest stories was about the poet Caedmon, actually a cowherd working for a monastery. As the story is told by Bede (often known as the venerable Bede), a devout and learned monk of Jarrow received a vision, about "A.D. 680, instructing him to sing a song about creation."[1] And for some four hundred years after that, the Anglo-Saxon people made parts of the Bible into song.

2. **Homilies (short sermons), metrical psalms (psalms in rhythmical form), and New Testament portions in English: A.D. 1000.** For several hundred years, from about 1000 to the time of John Wycliffe (1380), sermons and stories from the Bible appeared in various Anglo-Saxon dialects. As a result, the people became all the more eager to have the full Bible in their own tongue.

3. **First complete Bible in English: John Wycliffe, A.D. 1380.** One of the most important events in the history of the English Bible was the appearance of John Wycliffe's two translations, the first about 1380 (more like Latin), the second some twenty years later (closer to genuine English).

Deeply concerned about

---

[1] Bede, *Ecclesiastical History of the English Nation*, iv. 24, cited in F. F. Bruce, *History of the Bible in English*, 3rd ed. (Oxford: 1978), 2, 3.

corruption in the church and its leaders, Wycliffe determined to put the Bible into the hands of the people in a language they could understand. "No man is so rude a scholar," he said, "but that he might learn the words of the Gospel according to his simplicity." Whether clergy, knight, or commoner, "it helpeth Christian men to study the Gospel in that tongue in which they know best Christ's sentence."

Since there were no printing presses yet, copies of Wycliffe's English Bible were expensive. But the Word went out, and the people rejoiced.

The authorities, however, were not pleased. The Oxford Council of 1407 prohibited both the translation and the reading of any book of Scripture "composed in the time of the said John Wycliffe or later." Yet hungry souls were eager to circumvent the ban. At least one Bible has been preserved from that era, carrying an original date of MCCCCVIII (1408)— but with one *C* erased. This changed the date to 1308 and so presumably exempted that copy from the ban.

4. First printed English Bible: Tyndale's New Testament,

A.D. 1525. The first printed English New Testament was the work of William Tyndale. But translating and printing English Bibles was dangerous business. Even though he managed to flee to the continent, Tyndale was hunted down, strangled, then burned at the stake. A similar fate awaited others. Someone has noted that of all the early English Reformation translators, only one, Miles Coverdale, died in bed.

In the years following Tyndale, several other English Bibles appeared, preparing the way for the King James Bible of 1611. The Coverdale Bible was the first complete Bible to be printed in English, even though it was published in Zurich, Switzerland. Matthew's Bible, the Great Bible, the Geneva Bible, and the Bishops' Bible were all forerunners of the 1611 King James Version.

5. The Authorized King James Version of 1611. The Authorized Version, as the King James Version of 1611 is known in Britain, grew out of a confrontation with the Puritans, who claimed that the Bible quotations in the Anglican (Episcopalian)

Prayer Book were inaccurate.

A team of fifty-four translators was appointed, divided into six working groups. They were instructed to strike a middle course between the extreme Protestant and the extreme papist positions. And there were to be only explanatory notes in the margins, not the lively and sometimes bitter comment that had characterized the notes in some earlier Protestant versions.

Several times the completed translation underwent minor corrections (especially in 1769). Although the English language has changed a great deal since 1769, the spelling, punctuation, and phraseology of that 1769 revision continue to be the current form of the King James Version.

Understandably, then, late in the nineteenth century, a movement began to arise pressing for the revision of the King James Version. The result was the Revised Version of the New Testament, appearing in 1881, and the Old Testament in 1885. The American edition, known as the American Standard Version, appeared in 1901, with American usage replacing the British English of the Revised Version. The appearance of the Revised Version (RV) marks the beginning of the era of modern translations. But the King James Version has demonstrated remarkable staying power in spite of the many versions that have continued to appear since the RV was published. ⋏

· ·

 # Memory Focus

"Then he said to them, 'These are my words that I spoke to you while I was still with you—that everything written about me in the law of Moses, the prophets and the psalms must be fulfilled" (Luke 24:44, NSRV).

· ·

 # Into the Bible

2. **Keeping the Word of God Up-to-date.** It would be easy to think that translators simply translate a text from one language into another. But they also have to translate within a language when changes take place over a period of time. On the worksheet provided by your teacher, you will find a line-by-line comparison of three different English versions of the Lord's Prayer, one from an Anglo-Saxon

version at the time of King Alfred (A.D. 900), one from John Wycliffe (A.D. 1380), and one from the American Standard Version of 1901. Use your own modern version to add a fourth line for each phrase of the Lord's Prayer listed.

 # Projects

1. **A Bible for People Who Can't Read.** Imagine living in a time and place when ordinary people could not read and did not have their own Bibles. Choose one of the following stories, and make it come alive for people who can't read. Compose a song, write a poem, or write and act out a dramatic skit. Form a group with some of your classmates. Think of doing your project in a way that would make it easy for a nonreader to remember it.

   A. The Fall (Genesis 3)
   B. The sacrifice of Isaac (Genesis 22)
   C. The prodigal son (Luke 15:11-32)
   D. The ten virgins (Matthew 25:1-13)
   E. Healing the man born blind (John 9)

2. **Worshiping God in Another Language.** Find a Christian whose original language is something other than English. Ask that person to describe for you what it felt like to pray in English for the first time. Write a brief report to share with the class. If English was not or is not your mother tongue, describe your own feelings of trying to pray in a foreign language.

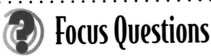 # Focus Questions

1. How would you feel if one of your classmates or someone you know claimed to have had a vision from God? Would you be likely to believe it? Why? or Why not?
2. Ellen White said her writings did not belong in the Bible. Why do you think she felt that way?
3. What do Christians mean when they say the Bible is true?
4. How important is it for a Christian to be able to read? If you couldn't read, how would you grow spiritually?
5. Why do some older Christians resist modern translations of the Bible? Is there danger in changing translations too quickly? Is there danger in not changing translations quickly enough?

ACTION

Knowing what to do must be translated into doing what you know
(The Daily Walk).

The Bible: Its Versions

**Lesson Scriptures: John 1:1-3;
                       Matthew 6:9-13**

If you use any other Bible than the King James Version, you could lose your faith!"

Ever hear a warning like that? It's not hard to find people who feel that way about changing Bibles, and it's a feeling that has deep roots.

If God doesn't change, His Word shouldn't change either. If someone tinkers with the Bible, how can we trust anything it says? That's the logic. And that's why some people cling to a Bible they don't understand rather than accept one that has changed, even if the changes make it easier to understand. As the title of a little book

defending the Bible puts it: *God Wrote Only One Bible*.

In the last hundred years, dozens of new translations of the Bible have appeared. Are they safe to use?

Actually, the King James translators themselves said good things about the value of *all* Bible translations. In their preface, "The Translators to the Readers," they said, "We affirm and avow, that the very meanest translation of the Bible in English . . . containeth the word of God, nay, is the word of God." [1]

The "meanest" translation? Is that the nastiest? Hardly. A good dictionary will suggest some other older meanings that would be much better, such as

---

[1] Cited in Ira M. Price, *The Ancestry of Our English Bible*, 3rd ed. (New York: Harper and Row, 1956), 273.

"humblest," "poorest," or even "lowest in quality." Already you sense one reason why new translations become necessary: The meanings of words change, even within a language. That's mean, isn't it?

Knowing how and why different versions of the Bible have come about helps us use them. Some believers are too quick to change to the new; others don't want to change at all. What we want to do here is learn enough about translations that we can receive help from both old and new.

In all translations, it is quite clear that the important things about God never change. He is love. It's not a love that shrugs or winks at sin. No. It's a love that hates sin so much that God was willing to come in human flesh, living and dying to save sinners.

But the message of love has to come in our language. That's the reason for the Bible in the first place and also the reason why people are eager to translate it. Something inside us wants to *understand* God's message. Still, almost every time a new translation appears, some will fight against the new and those eager for the new, fight against the old. That tension is worth remembering whenever anyone is tempted to get too excited about the old or the new.

NEW TRANSLATIONS: A STRUGGLE OVER CHANGE

You're reading this lesson in English. But imagine what would happen to you and your family if you moved to Russia or China or to any place where no one else spoke English. After two hundred years or so, what language would your descendants be speaking?

At first, your transplanted families would try very hard to keep their mother tongue alive, even making English-only rules for home. But the children learn the new language at school and at play. Even the adults have to learn it for work and shopping. By the time the kids grow up, English could be only a faint memory. The old folks can still speak it; the children might still understand it; but for the children of the children, it's as good as dead. The new language has won.

Something like that happened to the Jews when they left their homeland in Palestine. The destruction of Jerusalem in 586 B.C. marked the beginning of the Exile. Many Jews were carried off to Babylon, hundreds of miles away. That was the beginning of what is known as the Jewish Diaspora, a scattering of the Jews to foreign lands. Many of those Jews never returned home. Instead, large Jewish settlements sprang up on foreign soil. Babylon and Alexandria in Egypt became home for many Diaspora Jews.

These Jews discovered that their native Hebrew was dying out. Even when they lived together in tightly knit communities, they still began to adopt the language of the land in which they now lived. After Alexander of Macedonia conquered the Persian Empire in 331 B.C., the Greek language was used everywhere. Replacing Aramaic as the international language, Greek became the language of commerce and education. That's why the Jews of Alexandria knew Greek better than they knew their native Hebrew. And that brings us to the important first step in the process of translating God's Word into another language.

From Hebrew to Greek: The Greek Septuagint (LXX)

The Septuagint generally is seen as the first written translation of the Old Testament into another language. "The Letter of Aristeas" shows how Jews felt toward the new Greek translation of their Bible.

As the story goes, the Egyptian ruler, Ptolemy Philadelphus, wanted a copy of the Jewish Bible for the new library he was building in Alexandria. The king welcomed a team of

seventy-two Jewish scholars from Jerusalem. They began to translate the Hebrew Bible into Greek while enjoying the king's hospitality. Aristeas tells how the translators divided into working groups and then compared their results until everyone was happy. That use of committees is still the way the best modern translations are made today. But what is especially interesting for us is the obvious fear of change that cropped up when the new (changed!) translation was formally presented:

> After the books had been read, the priests and elders of the translators and the Jewish community and leaders of the people stood up and said, that since so excellent and sacred and accurate a translation had been made, it was only right that it should remain as it was and no alteration should be made in it. And when the whole company expressed their approval, they bade them pronounce a curse in accordance with their custom upon any one who should make any alteration either by adding anything or changing in any way whatever any of the words which had been written or making any omission. This was a very wise precaution to ensure **that the book might be preserved for all the future time unchanged.**[2]

Even though the old Hebrew form had been recast into a new Greek mold, it was the new Greek translation that was declared fixed for all time.

A modern Latin translation: Going back to the Hebrew original behind the Greek

Just as Alexander's Greek language became popular throughout his empire, so Latin, the language of the Romans, became popular when Rome took over from the Greeks. Though the two languages lived side-by-side for several hundred years, Latin gradually won out.

At the time of Jesus and the apostles, Greek was still popular, even under the Romans. John 19:20 tells us that the inscription on Jesus' cross was written in three languages: Hebrew (the local language); Latin (the language of the new Roman Empire); and Greek (the still-popular language from the previous empire.)

It's clear, however, that Greek was still number one, for the New Testament was written in Greek. Early Christians, along with Jesus and the apostles, often used the Greek Old Testament instead of the Hebrew. For many years, Greek continued to be the first language for sharing the gospel.

[2] Cited from R. H. Charles, ed., *The Apocrypha and Pseudepigrapha of the Old Testament*, vol. 2, *Pseudepigrapha* (Oxford, 1913), 121.

Latin replaced Greek in the Roman Empire, and just as Jews wanted a Greek Bible instead of the Hebrew, so Christians of the Roman Empire began asking for the Bible in Latin.

Gradually it happened. Translations in Old Latin sprang up all over the place. By A.D. 400, so many Old Latin translations of the Bible had appeared, some quite poorly done, that scholars and bishops longed for a good, reliable Latin translation that could be used everywhere. Jerome, a Christian monk with remarkable language skills, took on the task. He was so serious about his work that he went to Jerusalem and studied Hebrew under a Jewish rabbi.

When Jerome began working on his new official Latin translation (to be known as the Latin Vulgate), he discovered that the Greek Bible (LXX), from which the Old Latin had been translated, often differed from the Hebrew. As a scholar, he decided to base his new translation on the original Hebrew instead of the Greek. The result was a firestorm of protest in the church, for Jerome's Vulgate added to, deleted from, and made other changes to the familiar Bible.

Because he was basing his translation on the Hebrew, *not* the Greek, he *left out* anything in the Greek that wasn't in the Hebrew and *added* anything from the Hebrew that wasn't in the Greek!

Church members were outraged and heaped abuse on Jerome for changing the Bible. He took their insults with something less than good grace, denouncing his critics as "two-legged asses," to mention just one spicy example.

Again, as in the days of Aristeas, people didn't want to go back to the *original* Bible if it wasn't the same as their *familiar* Bible. "What we know is what we want," they said. "Don't change it."

Reformation Bibles: Forward to the language of the people, back to the language of the originals

Just as the Greek Septuagint had won its way over the Hebrew, so Jerome's Latin Vulgate eventually won over the Septuagint. But as the world moved toward the Reformation awakening, Latin wasn't the everyday language anymore. The people needed the Word of God in their own language. But

the church resisted. As long as the Bible was in Latin, the church could control the truth. The result was deadly.

William Tyndale, translator of the first printed English New Testament, once retorted to a clergyman who wanted to keep the Bible from ordinary people: "If God spare my life, ere many years I will cause a boy that driveth a plough shall know more of the Scripture than thou doest."[3]

As the Reformers struggled to give the Bible back to the people, they stood firm for two key principles that the official church had long resisted:

A. The Bible must be in the hands of the common people in a language they can understand.

B. New translations must be based on the best manuscripts in the original languages, rather than on the Latin.

Even as new Bibles appeared in the original languages, Latin often held the upper hand. In one Bible, for example, printed in Spain, 1514–17, the Old Testament was printed in three parallel columns, Hebrew, Latin, and Greek. The editor explained that the Latin was in the most important position, in the middle between the Hebrew and Greek, just as Jesus had been crucified between two thieves![4]

Again, it was clear that church people preferred the familiar over the original if the original was not familiar to them. No, it's nothing new to hear people defend their familiar version as though it were the original. It happened when people loved the Septuagint, again when they loved the Vulgate, and it happens still among those who love the King James Version of 1611.

GOOD REASONS FOR TRANSLATING THE BIBLE

In contrast with Muslims, who believe their sacred Koran is only inspired in its original Arabic language, Christians have the example of Jesus and His apostles, who used the Greek Bible, a translation of the original Hebrew.

Now, translation from one

---

[3] Price, 244.

[4] Price, 36.

language to another means change. But Christians believe the Holy Spirit can bless the change and keep the meaning faithful so that more people can hear God's voice in Scripture. In fact, when we summarize the four major reasons why new translations are good, we discover that they all have something to do with the desire to share God's Word with people.

1. A new translation makes it possible to share the gospel with PEOPLE WHO SPEAK A DIFFERENT LANGUAGE from the original language or the language in which the Bible has been available.

2. A new translation makes it possible to share the gospel more effectively with PEOPLE WHOSE LANGUAGE HAS CHANGED OVER TIME.

3. A new translation can take advantage of the DISCOVERY OF BETTER AND MORE ANCIENT MANUSCRIPTS.

4. A new translation can take advantage of RECENT ARCHAEOLOGICAL DISCOVERIES THAT EXPLAIN STRANGE BIBLICAL WORDS AND CUSTOMS.

We could give many illustrations for each one of these four points. But we will focus here on item 3, the discovery of more and better manuscripts.

WHEN SCRIBES COPY A MANUSCRIPT BY HAND

Generally, the older the manuscript, the better it is. It's closer to the original and generally hasn't been copied so often. But there are exceptions, for a careless scribe early in the process can mean that an old manuscript may not be as good as a newer one copied by careful scribes all the way along.

Every time a manuscript is copied, however, the possibility of error increases. And once an error is made and passed on in the new copy, it isn't easy to put it right again. Having good manuscripts helps. But sometimes when the paper trail is thin, it's almost impossible to tell what should have been there in the first place. The following are some of the more common events that can change a manuscript. Most of them are accidental, though sometimes scribes will try to correct a manuscript if they think they know what the manuscript should say. Usually, however,

65

such well-meaning scribes simply make matters worse.

Many ancient manuscripts were discovered in the nineteenth century. Often, they had been tucked away in some dark storeroom or library. All modern translations make active use of these manuscript discoveries. Only the New King James Version does not use any of these discoveries out of a desire to remain true to the KJV translation.

WRONG WORD DIVISIONS

For a period of time, Greek manuscripts were written in all capitals (Uncials) and with no division between the words. The well-known example in English is the following:

HEISNOWHERE

In this instance, two possible meanings exist for the same set of letters. The same is true of the phrases below related to Revelation 22:14:

1. hoi poiountes tas entolas autou
2. hoi plunontes tas stolas auton

The first translates as "who keep his commandments," the second one as "who wash their robes." Even though the Greek

sounds and looks alike, the English is very different.

In this case, both versions make good sense and help us understand the gospel. Good manuscripts support both sides, though some Adventists become alarmed that commandment keeping may be lost when a translation chooses the robe-washing option. But it is hard to see how such a translation could undermine the importance of commandment keeping, especially when the call to obedience is so very clear in many New Testament passages.

UNWARRANTED CHANGES IN TRANSLATIONS

Deliberate doctrinal changes. One of the best-known examples in modern translations is the change made by Jehovah's Witnesses in John 1:1. The KJV translation, followed by most modern versions, is: "In the beginning was the Word and the Word was with God and the Word was God." The *New World Translation*, published by Jehovah's Witnesses, reads that "the Word was a god." Since Jehovah's Witnesses do not believe that Jesus is God in the fullest sense, John 1:1 was a problem for their theology.

Some scholars have even suggested that John 1:1 was *the* real reason behind the *New World Translation.*

Unwarranted or deliberate changes like this are most unfortunate but are also very uncommon. From the original writer to later copyists to modern translators, consistent efforts were made to faithfully preserve the inspired messages. It is reassuring to know that even though some copying or translation errors have occurred, the essential themes of God's Word have not been changed.

WHICH TRANSLATION IS BEST?

When trying to decide which translation is best, the very next question is, Best for what? Different versions are used in different ways. But to find an answer, we need to ask several other questions first. The important ones are:

1. **Does the translation present a *FORMAL* equivalence (literal, word-for-word interpretation of the original) or *DYNAMIC* equivalence (does it seek to have the same effect on the new reader that the original**

had on the first reader)? The formal translators seek to find the closest word or phrase to match the word or phrase in the original language. The New American Standard Bible is perhaps the best modern example of a Bible that seeks a formal, word-for-word equivalence. A word-for-word translation can be especially helpful as a study Bible. The disadvantage of the word-for-word translation is that it can produce a heavy, wooden translation that doesn't "sing" in the new language.

At the other end of the spectrum is the translation method that seeks to produce the same dynamic effect on the new reader that the original had on the original hearers. Thus the translator has more freedom. The disadvantage is that the new can differ dramatically from the original. On the positive side, readability gets high marks. J. B. Phillips' New Testament paraphrase is a good example of a dynamic translation. Phillips often expands the biblical text to make it more readable. That's why his version is so good for devotional reading.

2. **Was the translation produced by a committee or by an individual?** Generally, broadly based committees offer a much more consistent translation than one produced by an individual. Most of the major modern translations were prepared by committees. Phillips' New Testament, Kenneth Taylor's Living Bible, and William Barclay's New Testament are some of the better-known translations by individuals. Taylor's paraphrase, in particular, has been criticized for some of its special readings. While his Living Bible is very readable, it also reflects Taylor's personal theology in ways that are often misleading.

3. **Was the translation produced by some special interest group?** We have already noted that the *New World Translation,* produced by Jehovah's Witnesses, is driven by the desire to say that Jesus was not fully divine.

4. Finally, we need to point out **the technical difference between a *version* and a *translation,*** though the words are often used interchangeably. In brief, a version is simply a revision of a previous translation. The KJV, for example, was technically a version based on the Bishop's Bible of 1572.

By contrast, the New International Version (NIV) is a brand-new translation, not tied at all to the KJV tradition. The Jerusalem Bible is a totally new translation by Roman Catholic scholars.

CONCLUSION

Which Bible is for you? One that warms your heart and feeds your soul. You might want more than one translation, for each translation is actually a mini-commentary. A Bible should encourage you to think, to act, to worship. Some will do a better job at helping you think, others at helping you worship. But it is also helpful to remember the good words of the KJV translators. "We affirm and avow, that the very meanest translation of the Bible in English . . . containeth the word of God, nay, is the word of God." Amen. ⋏

A COMPARISON OF BIBLE VERSIONS

Bible versions or translations can be classified into one of these three groups:

Formal: A WORD FOR WORD translation as close to original language as possible.
Emphasis: Literal exactness.

Dynamic: A translation that expresses the thought of the original language PHRASE BY PHRASE.
Emphasis: Accuracy and readability.

Paraphrase: A highly interpretive version of the original language expressed PARAGRAPH BY PARAGRAPH.
Emphasis: Relevance and interest.

FORMAL	DYNAMIC	PARAPHRASE
New American Standard		
King James Version		
New King James Version		
Revised Standard Version		
New International Version		
New English Bible		
The Jerusalem Bible		
Phillips Modern English		
The Living Bible		
The Clear Word		

 **Memory Focus**

"Above all, you must understand that no prophecy of Scripture came about by the prophet's own interpretation. For prophecy never had its origin in the will of man, but men spoke from God as they were carried along by the Holy Spirit" (2 Peter 1:20, 21, NIV).

 # Into the Bible

1. Compare the Lord's Prayer of Matthew 6:9-13 in the King James Version or in the New King James Version with any other modern version. Answer the following questions:

   A. What one major difference did you discover between the KJV or NKJV and other English translations?
   B. Do the footnotes or margin in your Bible offer any explanation for the difference?
   C. Is it possible that part of the Lord's Prayer came from 1 Chronicles 29:10, 11?
   D. Which do you think is the right way to say the Lord's Prayer? Why?

2. Compare the famous virgin birth passages of Isaiah 7:14 and Matthew 1:23, first in the King James Version or New King James Version and then in other modern translations. Read both chapters in context; then answer the following questions:

   A. If you were hearing Isaiah in Isaiah's own day, who do you think you would understand the "young woman" or "virgin" to be?
   B. You could find several modern versions that change *virgin* of Isaiah 7:14 to *young woman* or something similar, but can you find any modern version of Matthew 1 that does *not* teach a virgin birth?
   C. Does the doctrine of the virgin birth need to be clear in both Isaiah and Matthew, or is Matthew enough? Read the explanation of Isaiah 7:14 in the *Seventh-day Adventist Bible Commentary*.

3. Compare Matthew 12:46-50; Mark 3:31-35; and Luke 8:19-21 in a modern version of the Bible. Can you guess why some modern versions omit verse 47 from Matthew 12? Does the omission of that verse from Matthew make any difference in what you believe about God?

· ·

 # Projects

1. **Be a Scribe.** Your teacher will give instructions for an experiment on sending a message. The class will then discuss how the process might have worked during the copying and translating of Bible manuscripts.

Discuss, also, whether the presence of the Holy Spirit would have changed the results of the process of copying and translating the Bible transcripts.

2. **Dynamic and Formal Equivalence.** Compare several versions of John 1:1-3, indicating which ones are closer to formal and which ones closer to dynamic equivalence. Which one is the clearest? Which one sounds the best?

3. **Modernizing Our Words.** Turn to a familiar story or passage in the KJV, and make a list of KJV words that seem curious to you or that you simply don't understand. Then list the new word as found in the NKJV. How do the new words affect your attitude toward the Bible?

 # Focus Questions

1. Are there some aspects of your religious experience in which you welcome change? Are there some aspects in which you want no change at all? Why?

2. Which do you think would be more helpful: To memorize a Scripture from a classic version that you don't quite understand or from a modern one that is different but quite understandable? Explain.

3. If an atheist mechanic can fix a car without being a Christian, can an atheist translator translate the Bible? Why?

4. What is your favorite Bible translation? What would you think of having two Bibles, a "formal equivalence" Bible for careful study and a "dynamic equivalence" Bible for devotional reading?

5. In light of all the modern versions, what should we do about memorizing Scripture? Should we try to standardize one Bible for church? Should we all just memorize from our favorite translations? Should we just give up memorizing?

COURAGE

A person must be big enough to admit his mistakes, smart enough to profit from them, and strong enough to correct them *(Quips and Quotes).*

The Bible: Its Study

Lesson Scripture: Proverbs 3:1-8

WHY STUDY THE BIBLE?

Why do you study the Bible?

If someone surprised you with that question, and you had to give a quick answer off the top of your head (without really thinking too much about it), what would be your response? On the worksheet provided by your teacher, indicate which statement would come the closest to your reason.

Now go back to that same list, and give each item a score from 1 to 10 in response to the question: How good a reason is this for studying the Bible? A 10 would be a good reason, a 1 would be a poor reason.

But now let's get really honest and personal. If you're not spending as much time with the Bible as you think you should (and you have *lots* of company if you're not), to what extent do the reasons listed on the worksheet apply to you? Give a 10 if it's a "bull's-eye" on down to a 1 if it doesn't apply at all. Record your responses on the worksheet provided.

THE DEVOTIONAL HABIT

When you were very small, you learned lots of things to do and lots not to do. Those things became habits. You didn't even think about them anymore.

Some habits last as long as we live. But as we grow older, we are more likely to keep the good habits if we have good reasons for them. So even though it's obviously good to have good

habits, good habits are even better if we know why we have them. The goal of this lesson is to help you find good reasons for the good habit of studying the Bible. If you already have the habit, fine. You can add more good reasons for keeping it. If you don't have the habit, now is the time to start.

If you read Ellen White's little book *Steps to Christ* and make a list of the positive things you can do as a Christian, you will likely come up with a basic list of three: pray, study, and share. For some reason, it's easy to think of those things as three separate requirements that we're supposed to do just to keep God happy or in order to be saved. If we do them just to keep God off our backs, rather than for what they mean to us, our devotional lives will be a lot more like work and less like having good times with a friend. The goal of this lesson is to find ways to make Bible study mean something to you personally, not just something that you check off because it is required.

Even though this lesson focuses on Bible study, we also need to look at the two other tools that go along with the Bible if you really want to have a healthy devotional life. Devo-

tional life? Yes. That refers to a time (or even better, an attitude) when you and God are on the same wavelength, when you are talking, sharing, listening to each other. There are many purposes for studying the Bible that aren't directly devotional. But since the devotional use of the Bible is probably the most important one for Christians, we should consider it first.

Now, back to those two tools that go along with the Bible in your devotional life. First, your head, or the power of reason. Believe it or not, your head is indispensable if you're going to study the Bible. But it's not safe to use your head unless you have the other essential tool to go along with it. We'll talk a bit more later about how dangerous it is to use your head without the other tool.

Prayer is that other essential tool. But it's not the tool we're after; it's a person, the Holy Spirit. The tool is only a means to get the Spirit on board.

The Spirit makes it safe to use our heads when we study the Bible. But He only comes by our invitation.

Now you're ready for a lively, three-way conversation: your Bible, you (your head), and the Spirit. The Bible doesn't jump into your life with the answers. It sits quietly on your table waiting to be read. When you open it, you'll find it bristling with all kinds of good things: stories, laws, songs, prayers, letters, wise sayings, and visions. You have to use your head to know where to start. But can you trust your head? If you have invited the Spirit to be there, you can. But only then. And it's not only important to have the Spirit there; you have to remember He's there. That way, you won't be tempted to do anything sneaky with the Bible. No, the Spirit keeps you honest. If you don't invite the Spirit, it would be easy for sin (selfishness) to make you study the Bible for the wrong reason.

Some Christians seem to think that you don't need your brain to interpret the Bible. Some seem to think that prayer is a substitute for using your mind. But either of those two approaches can lead to some hefty tensions between your mind and the Bible or between your mind and the Spirit. The proper use of prayer enables you to use your mind more, not less, because the Spirit guides you according to the principles of God's kingdom. You're not left to follow your own selfish thoughts.

The Bible, your mind, and the Spirit all have a special work to do. And when all three are doing their jobs, they get along just fine.

STUDYING THE BIBLE: THE HOW, THE WOW, AND THE DO
Different Methods for Different Purposes

By dividing the essential aspects of the Christian life into three categories, the How, the Wow, and the Do, we can look at how the Bible can be most useful for each. But first let's summarize what is meant by each of the three:

The How. Under this heading are included the various ways of studying and analyzing the Bible as a book, as history, as literature. Who wrote what to whom and when? Where did they live? Customs, culture, language, manuscripts, translations are all part of the How.

The Wow. This is the worship side of our Christian life. It has to do with awe, wonder, joy, and fear (reverence) in God's presence. It is our personal encounter with Christ as our risen Lord and Saviour. When we are in the business of appreciating the Wow, we are so close to Him, we often won't dare ask about the How. We simply let ourselves be overwhelmed by His glory and power. The psalms and prayers of the Bible fit in here. Here is where we sing praises, raise our voices in thanksgiving, and cry out our complaints and laments. Yes, the Wow includes our complaints. Sometimes things are so bad that God is the only one who will listen to our troubles.

The Do. This is the hands-on part of the Christian life. Here we learn about sharing with others what God has done for us and about helping others who are in trouble. Here we decide what we should and shouldn't do. We seek God for guidance and then get out and do what we believe He has asked us to do.

A healthy Christian life will include a balanced diet of the How, the Wow, and the Do. If we concentrate on the How only, we may lose the sense of wonder that motivates us to worship God. If we only hear the Wow, we will find it harder to make decisions based on the Bible. If we focus only on the Do, we may not be able to understand the stories or the laws that tell us to

do, and we may not feel the fire in our bones that comes from the Wow.

Some ways of reading or studying the Bible will focus mostly on one of the three aspects; others will mix and match the parts. If we are really honest, however, every method should probably include at least a small touch of all three elements.

BASIC BIBLE-STUDY TOOLS

Listed below are some standard reference works that can help you study and understand the Bible:

A. **Concordance.** Good for doing word studies based on the way a word is used in the Bible.
B. **Bible Dictionary.** Contains articles on Bible characters, places, and names. A good dictionary will include an article on every important word, person, place, and concept found in the Bible.
C. **Atlas.** A good atlas will give you maps and brief articles explaining the various maps in connection with the Bible stories. It helps to have a feel for chronology (time references) so that you can find the right map to match

the Bible passage. An atlas might help you with chronology, as well.

D. **Commentary.** Commentaries will help you interpret a passage in a particular book. A one-volume commentary gives you very brief comments on any particular passage. There are some commentaries, like the seven-volume *Seventh-day Adventist Bible Commentary,* that cover the entire Bible. A commentary on a particular book can be very helpful. Very sophisticated commentaries expect the reader to know Greek and Hebrew, the languages in which the Bible was originally written.

PLANNING YOUR OWN BIBLE STUDY

1. **The Story of Jesus.** Since Jesus is the clearest revelation of God, a generous dose of the Gospels is terribly important as the first step in any Bible-study plan.

2. **Bible Characters.** Studying important Bible characters one by one can be very revealing. Make a list of the things you like and don't like about each one. Make a list of the things they teach you about God. Make a list of the things you find encouraging or discouraging about each one.

3. **Prayers of the Bible.** Start making a master list of the important prayers in the Bible. Comment on your list as to whether they are cries for help, words of thanksgiving or praise, or prayers of complaint. Jesus' prayers are especially interesting.

4. **Books of the Bible.** This is a project that will keep you going for a while. You can outline each book. After reading and studying each book, it is helpful to give a one-line summary for each. Don't find a summary in a book. Make your own.

5. **Great Miracles of the Bible.** This is the kind of study that will help you feel the Wow. You might want to start looking for miracles (little and big) in your life and in the lives of those around you. Making a list of those will help the Wow in your life too.

6. **Great Themes of the Bible.** The sky is the limit here. In fact, that may be the problem. You can start tracing ideas like forgiveness,

deliverance, hope, or faith. Sin, salvation, and atonement can be even more challenging. God's judgment and His second coming are also important themes. A Bible dictionary can get you started. A good topical Bible (such as *Nave's Topical Bible*) can also be a good place to start.

7. **Word Studies.** The concordance is the right tool here. The possibilities are so enormous that they could be discouraging. It's easy to chase rabbits instead of elephants when you're doing word studies. Still, they can be very helpful and interesting.

 # Memory Focus

"These things happened to them to serve as an example, and they were written down to instruct us, on whom the ends of the ages have come" (1 Corinthians 10:11, NRSV).

Into the Bible

1. **READING THE BIBLE FOR THE WOW**

   The word *reading* is used here rather than *studying* because the Wow is something that comes more naturally. Sometimes while you are studying the How, a Wow will come to you. Generally, however, the Wow will come from those passages that don't require a lot of interpreting but come rather naturally into our lives. Using a modern translation, read Psalms 23, 91, 98, and 150. Listen to your soul as you read. Give each psalm a rating of 1 to 10 on how much Wow it gave you. (Ten is the highest Wow.)

2. **STUDYING THE BIBLE FOR THE DO**

   Suppose you said you would do whatever the Bible tells you to do. If you just opened the Bible at random and read a command from God, would you do it? Let's try it out.

   A. **READ:** Using a modern version, read Proverbs 3:1-8. Make a list of

the things to do mentioned in these passages.

B. **PONDER:** Look at your list, and indicate which of these things you are ready to do immediately. If there are any commands you would find difficult to follow, briefly explain why.

The Bible is a great resource book. It is the test of all that we do and believe. But it's not enough to know the Bible; we need to know the God revealed in Jesus Christ (John 17:3). That's why the three-way conversation is so important. Your Bible, you, and the Spirit. By inviting God to be with you through His Spirit, you will get to know God.

 Projects

1. Establish a devotional plan for your life for a two-week period. Write out the length of each devotion, the time of day, and the nature of the activity (Bible reading, witnessing, sharing, etc.).
2. Write a report describing the features and uses of Bible commentaries.
3. Become familiar with using a Bible commentary, concordance, dictionary, and atlas by answering the questions on the worksheet provided by your teacher.
4. Read the "Introduction," pages v to xii, in *The Great Controversy.* Summarize what Ellen White says regarding the following issues:

   A. How did God go about writing the Bible?
   B. What is the purpose of the Bible?
   C. What guidelines should be followed in the study of the Bible?

 Focus Questions

1. How can the Bible become a more interesting and practical book to us?
2. What can a person do to establish a devotional pattern in his/her life?
3. Can the study of the Bible ever be a dangerous or wrong thing to do? Explain.
4. How can one know whether a certain interpretation of the Bible is right or wrong?
5. How important is it to share our faith and love for Christ with others? Is it necessary to talk about it, or can we just live our faith?
6. As we seek God for guidance in prayer and Bible study, how does He make His will known to us?

unit

2

God's Gifts: Creation and Salvation

Creation

Unit two explores some of the major worldviews of God and addresses the issues involved in the origin of all things. It reveals God's purpose for the Sabbath and analyzes the sin problem that resulted from Satan's destructive rebellion. This unit provides the good news that God indeed is in control, that He loves humankind with an infinite love, and that He has a plan that ensures eternal security for all that love Him.

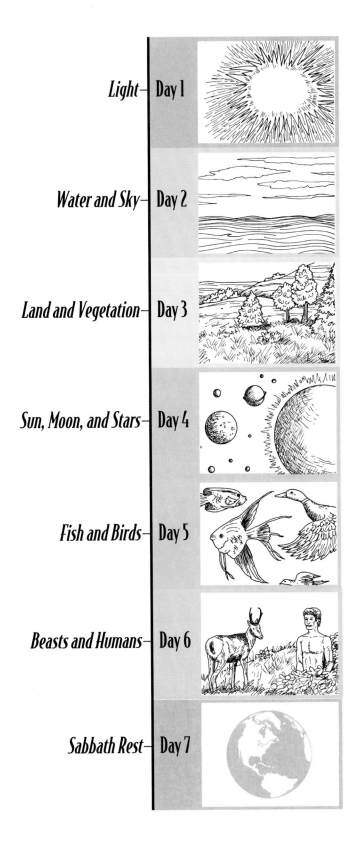

Light — Day 1

Water and Sky — Day 2

Land and Vegetation — Day 3

Sun, Moon, and Stars — Day 4

Fish and Birds — Day 5

Beasts and Humans — Day 6

Sabbath Rest — Day 7

INFINITY

If God was small enough for us to understand, He wouldn't be big enough
for us to worship *(Quips and Quotes)*.

lesson 8

The Creator: A Personal God

Lesson Scripture: Job 38:1-15

OD WHO?

The wail of sirens and the sharp crackle of a raging fire drew a crowd even at two o'clock in the morning. A firefighter brought out the sad news of a family trapped and three people dead.

"What a waste!" the firefighter said quietly. "Three lives, snuffed out forever."

"They're not really gone," said a man in a bathrobe; "they've just rejoined the universe. They've taken a different form now, but life never ends."

"I'm afraid you're wrong. This life is all there is," objected a woman holding a baby. "When a person dies, all that is left is what they have done on earth and those who remember them."

"But wait," a high-school freshman said. "What about heaven? Or hell? Doesn't God …"

"God who?" interrupted the woman. "There is no God. That's just a fairy tale your parents taught you."

"But what about . . ."

"I agree with you, kid," the firefighter spoke up. "I think there is a God. But I don't think He gets involved in little stuff like our everyday lives. He's out there, but He doesn't meddle in our world."

"Of course there is a God." The man in the bathrobe spoke again as he pointed to himself. "But He isn't out there; He's in here. He's part of us, and we are part of Him."

The memory of the firetrucks' wail accompanied

the high-school student as he walked away. *Everyone seems to believe something,* he thought. *What do I believe?*

Obviously, not everyone worships or believes in a god or gods in the same way. But deep down, everyone believes in something. Everyone has a "bottom line," something they put their ultimate faith in, even if it's the idea that there's nothing to have faith in.

Why are pain, suffering, and death in the picture? Are they just part of a natural, never-ending cycle of good and evil? Are they evidence that humans must evolve to an even higher state? Or are they the very real effects of sin, which has already been defeated by Christ and will someday be abolished forever?

These are the kinds of questions that human beings have struggled with since the beginning of time. We want to know how we got here, why we're here, who's in charge of things, and what will happen to us when we die. All through history, civilizations and peoples have come up with many different answers to these basic questions. Some of their answers can be found in cave paintings, in myths and legends, in music and art, and in organized systems of religion.

There are basically four major worldviews regarding who God is or isn't. They are:

➤ Atheism

➤ Deism

➤ Theism (comes from the Greek term *theos,* which means "God")

➤ Pantheism

Almost everyone accepts one of these belief systems or worldviews about the nature of the universe and our place in it. Let's look at each one more carefully.

FOUR MAJOR WORLDVIEWS

1. ATHEISM

Atheism is the belief that no God exists. There is no divine creator. Even further, there are no supernatural powers of any kind at work in the universe. The universe evolved over a vast amount of time and keeps itself going by natural processes. The universe is just there. When we die, our bodies decompose into their various elements, and our minds simply cease to exist.

2. DEISM

Think of deism as a form of Christianity without the miracles. A deist would agree that there was a creator, but that creator does not interfere with his creation. God is to the world what a master mechanic is to his machine; he created it, set it in motion according to certain laws, and then stepped back and let it function on its own.

Deists and atheists agree that there is a world in which there is no supernatural activity, no unexplainable "miracles." Some deists even believe in a kind of evolution, where God provided the initial spark of life, then let natural evolution take over from there.

Though most deists reject the Bible as the inspired Word of God, they do accept its moral teaching as a standard for living. Stories about miracles, such as the parting of the Red Sea or the raising of Lazarus, they believe, are no different from the legends of Hercules or King Arthur.

3. THEISM

Christians are theists. Theists believe in a personal, infinite God who created the world, keeps it going, and sometimes intervenes in human affairs.

Theists accept the God revealed in the Old and New Testaments—a God who hears and answers prayers, who cares about the life of each individual, and who intervenes to help and communicate with them. God created the universe to run according to natural and moral laws that are still in effect. He is involved with His creation, but He is not part of it, any more than an artist is part of a painting he or she has completed.

4. PANTHEISM

Pantheism is the belief that god is the universe, and the universe is god. Pantheists believe that god flows through all created things and is the force holding the universe together. All things, humans, trees, oceans, stars, and even insects are divine because they are part of god. Since everything is god, everything is worshiped; only good exists.

In pantheism, god is the life force of the universe. This energy or force flows through the universe. It is the goal of pantheists to be united with this divine life force.

Another belief held by pantheists is that they have lived before and they will live again in a different form. In fact, they believe that each time they die they are reborn over and over again. This is known as reincarnation and is a belief commonly held in Eastern religions. A new form of pantheism, commonly known as New Age, includes the belief in supernatural powers and "higher" spirits that are channeled or communicated with.

Of all these major worldviews, theism offers the most sensible answers to life's questions. Of course, the Bible paints a vivid portrait of a powerful, personal God. But even outside the Bible, there is evidence all around us supporting a theistic worldview. This evidence can be placed in three categories:

1. *The human need to worship.* Humans have a natural tendency to search for a power beyond themselves to worship. Every civilization in recorded history has worshiped something—the sun, the stars, stone carvings, imaginary gods. This quest for a relationship with a higher power seems a built-in part of human nature.

2. *The design of nature.* The modern world is powered by an astonishing array of marvelous human inventions, from cars to lasers, VCRs to heart-lung machines. But none of them come close to the intricate design of a flower, a bird, or a human brain. The intelligent design of the world is powerful proof of a personal creator.

3. *A true Christian life.* Perhaps the greatest miracle of all, and the strongest evidence for the truth of theism, is how it affects a person's life. Can any other worldview transform a cruel, self-centered egotist into a loving, selfless giver?

·Ever since sin separated us from God, we've been groping for answers to life's basic questions. Why are we here? What's the purpose of our lives? How will it all end? For many of us, the idea of a personal God who wants to befriend us, guide us, and save us is appealing or even frightening. It implies that we can't make it on our own or perhaps God requires too much of us. It's tempting to believe that there is no God and that our only responsibility is to keep on evolving as best we can. Or that we are all part of the god-like force that flows through created things. Or that, if there is a God, He's so uninvolved that He doesn't really matter, so all we can do is be the best people we can be.

But comforting untruths are still untruths in the end. Jesus said the truth would make us free, and that, really, is the greatest comfort of all. ⚊

Memory Focus

"In the beginning was the Word, and the Word was with God, and the Word was God. He was with God in the beginning. Through him all things were made; without him nothing was made that has been made" (John 1:1-3, NIV).

. . . .

 # Into the Bible

1. How do each of the following verses oppose the beliefs of pantheism?
   A. Job 38:4-6, NIV
   B. Isaiah 44:24, NIV
   C. Hebrews 3:4, NIV
2. How does each of the following verses oppose the beliefs of deism?
   A. John 3:16
   B. Matthew 14:13-21
   C. Genesis 12:7
3. What does the Bible say about the human need to worship?
   Romans 1:20-25; Acts 17:23
4. What is the best evidence of a personal God?
   John 3:16; 1 John 4:10-19
5. Describe what kind of friend God is. Base your response on the following verses:
   Romans 8:31-39; Hebrews 13:5; Psalm 91:10; John 14:1-3; John 17:3
6. What does nature reveal about the character and activity of God? Read the following texts, and summarize:
   A. Psalm 19:1-6   D. Isaiah 44:24
   B. Psalm 33:6   E. Isaiah 48:13
   C. Isaiah 40:25-31   F. Job 38:1-7

 **Projects**

1. Identify the worldview held by each person in the introduction to the lesson:
   A. Firefighter
   B. Man in bathrobe
   C. Woman holding baby
   D. High-school freshman
2. Which of the three evidences of a personal God described in the lesson is the strongest? Why? Is there other evidence outside of the Bible that supports belief in a personal God?
3. How do each of the four worldviews explain the origin and nature of the universe?
4. Choose one of the worldviews, and describe what it teaches about:
   A. evil
   B. suffering
   C. death and afterlife
   D. worship

 **Focus Questions**

1. Why do you think that everyone needs to believe in something?
2. Which picture of God is more attractive, theism's or deism's?
3. What is the strongest evidence of a personal God?
4. Why are there so many different views of God and the universe?
5. Which of the four worldviews would be the most comfort to someone whose friend had recently died? Why?

TRUST

If the Bible is mistaken in telling us from where we come,
how can we trust it to tell us where we are going? *(Quips and Quotes)*

Our World: Design or Chance?

Lesson Scriptures: Genesis 1-2; Psalm 33:6-9

of!" Jon staggered back a step as Eric's shoulder caught him in the chest. He swiped at the basketball, but Eric was already past him with a clear shot at the basket. With a last-second lunge, Jon jumped high enough to tip Eric's shot away.

"Boy, you sure take this game seriously," Eric shouted as he raced after the ball.

"Me?" Jon asked, one step behind Eric. "You turn into some kind of animal on the court." Eric grabbed the ball and spun around for a quick jump shot. Jon's hand swung up too late. *Swish*!

"Let's take a break for a minute," Jon said. He caught the ball on its first bounce and leaned against the gym wall. Before he could slide down the wall to the floor, Eric grabbed the ball away. "Aw, come on," Jon said, "rest."

"You rest," Eric said as he dribbled in for another shot. "I need the practice."

"Do you always have to be the best?" Jon groaned.

Eric banked one off the glass. "Hey, that's life. You know, the 'survival of the fittest.' What else is there?"

"What do you mean?"

Eric stopped dribbling for a second. "You only get one shot at life. You have to be the best you can be. You have to be the best, make the most money, have the nicest car, live in the greatest house. What else is there?"

Jon snorted. "I get it. Who-

ever dies with the most toys, wins."

"Exactamundo," Eric answered. He swished another one.

"Wins what?" Jon asked quietly.

Eric grabbed the bouncing ball. "Huh?"

"What do you win?" Jon repeated. "So you have all the best stuff when you die—you're still dead! Is that it? Is that all there is to life?"

"That's it," Eric said. "Give it all you got now, cause you don't get no more. What else is there? We evolved from monkeys, who evolved from pond slime. What else could there be? Come on, let's play another game."

Jon just sat there for a minute. "Is that really it? Is that all life really amounts to? I guess if you really believe that you descended from monkeys, that's all there can be."

He hopped up. "Take the ball out, hoop brain. No relative of pond slime is going to beat me."

THE ORIGIN OF LIFE

People who have questions about the origin of life usually end up with one of two answers: either life was created by a divine being (God), or life developed naturally, by itself. It either happened by design or by chance.

Two theories, creation and evolution, are the major models of the origin of life. Usually, people think of creationism as being totally unscientific and evolution as being totally nonreligious. But that's not accurate.

We say that something is scientific when it is testable and repeatable, when anyone can repeat the test and get the same results. The law of gravity is a good example. You and I or anyone can drop an object and test the law of gravity. And no matter what we drop or where we drop it, the law of gravity will take effect in some way. Scientifically speaking, everything is explainable by natural means— if we understand it correctly.

We say something is religious when it depends on a force beyond nature (supernatural) to explain the world around us. Instead of being able to prove that such things are correct, they are accepted on faith. That means we believe in a supernatural being. We believe in God.

A good example of that is

the story of manna falling from heaven, as recorded in the book of Exodus. When the children of Israel needed food, it appeared like dew on the grass. Obviously, there is no scientific explanation for a thing like that—at least not at the present time. The fact that it happened, and how it happened, can only be accepted as supernatural, a miracle.

THE THEORY OF EVOLUTION

Evolution teaches that life began from a mixture of nonliving chemicals when, completely by chance, those chemicals were combined in just the right way. The result: all life forms evolved from that original life. These life forms developed new organs and abilities as needed to survive.

Are those ideas scientific? It is scientific that nonliving chemicals are essential for life. Science has never developed a rational model that shows how those chemicals could have combined in the right way by chance. No one can duplicate it. The chances are greater that an explosion in an auto parts store would create a new car than life would have developed by chance! That is why evolution demands millions and even billions of years to explain the origin of life. When one is depending on chemicals to accidentally get together, you have to leave a lot of time for that "accident" to happen!

The truth is, a person has to have faith in something that has never been observed or proven to believe in evolution. Evolution has to appeal to the "gods" of time, statistics, and human reason. Evolution is based on the theory that given enough time, millions or billions of years, evolution could happen.

It is scientific that all life on earth shares things in common. It can be shown that the structure of cells and the chemical makeup are very similar in all animals. Also, as evolution claims, it is true that animals evolve or adapt to survive.

However, scientists describe two types of evolution—macroevolution and microevolution.

MACROEVOLUTION

In macroevolution, life is seen as undergoing continual changes due to genetic mutations and external forces.

Mutations occur when radiation causes changes within the cells of a species. These changes cause differences. For example, a change of hair or eye color, a larger or smaller beak, or an increase or decrease in size. Also, with the struggle to survive, the weak mutations die. That leaves the surviving members of a species with the strong mutations.

According to macroevolution, with enough time, this kind of change allows a species to change so much that it becomes a different species altogether. For example, some scientists believe that today's birds are descendants of the dinosaurs. Those dinosaurs who mutated the ability to grow feathers and fly survived. The rest died off.

While many scientists believe that macroevolution gave us the many species of animals we find in our world, it is important to point out that macroevolution has never been witnessed. No transitional forms have ever been found. That is, no fossil or skeleton has been found that is halfway between a reptile and a bird.

Even if macroevolution is a process that takes millions of years, it is reasonable to assume that some species should be in this transitional form today. And nothing like that has been found.

MICROEVOLUTION

Microevolution occurs when a population of animals or plants are cut off from others of their kind. For example, the Galapagos Island iguanas. Iguanas, large lizards, inhabit much of South and Central America. But at some point in the past, a number of these reptiles found themselves on the Galapagos Islands, cut off from others of their kind.

Iguanas are typically land-dwelling lizards, living on insects. But as their usual food sources dried up, the iguanas on the Galapagos Islands found themselves trapped. In order to survive, they do something that iguanas nowhere else do. They dive underwater to find and eat the algae that is now their food. This adaption is called micro-evolution.

But notice that the iguanas did not develop wings and fly to another island to search for food. No animal has ever been observed to develop new organs or limbs in order to survive. If an animal were to actually develop new organs or limbs, this would be an example of macroevolution.

Macroevolution is a leap of faith. It requires a belief in transitional forms that no one has ever seen. Evolutionists have faith that these things could occur over millions of years.

So evolution is not, at its core, totally scientific. Evolutionists have to believe that certain things happened that have never been observed, things that really have no chance of happening.

The following summarizes beliefs generally held about evolution:

1. No superior power was involved with the origin of the earth or the universe.

2. All life originated by natural mechanical processes, completely by chance, that are capable of being explained by the laws of chemistry and physics.

3. Life began millions of years ago, and through macroevolution, all life forms today evolved from that original life. The mutation of new organs and abilities has allowed new species to survive.

4. All species continue to evolve and change, with the weak dying off and the strong surviving.

CREATIONISM

Is creationism completely religious? Creationists believe that a Higher Power, God, spoke physical matter into existence as He created the universe. Most creationists believe in microevolution, that living forms do change, but the change is limited and not progressive.

In addition, many creationists believe that the surface of the earth was drastically rearranged by the worldwide flood as described in Genesis, and many plant and animal species were destroyed at that time.

It does require faith to believe that God created the earth as recorded in the Bible. But it requires faith to believe in evolution's creation of life as well. Creationism is consistent with proven science when it teaches that living forms change

in only a limited way. Examples like the Galapagos iguana are common.

There is a lot of evidence that the surface of the earth has suffered a catastrophe like the Flood. While most evolutionists claim millions of years of time have produced the mountains and canyons of the earth, Creationists can point to scientific facts like these:

1. Seashells and rocks formed under water are found on many of the earth's mountains.

2. Many large rock formations have been identified as turbidites. Turbidites are formed by underwater mud slides. It has been shown that these can form quickly.

3. Many rock formations cover vast areas. The Morrison formation, in which many dinosaur fossils have been discovered, is found in most of the western United States. There is no evidence that the geological forces acting today could form such large deposits.

THEORIES OF CREATION

While most Christians believe in creationism, there are several different basic theories. These theories range from an attempt to blend creation with evolution to one in which God is not presented as the all-powerful Creator described in the Bible to a simple acceptance of the Bible only. The following is an overview of theories of creation held by creationists.

Theistic Evolution. This theory is probably the most widely held belief for the origin of life outside the belief in special creation. It seeks to blend the interpretations of modern science and evolution without

eliminating God totally from the process. In this theory, God created the first cells of life, then stepped back and allowed evolution to take over. God is not presented as the all-powerful Creator described in the Bible. In fact, this theory postulates that God is limited to the laws of nature rather than being their creator. In addition, the time frame in the Bible is rejected.

Deistic Evolution. In this theory, God created the first blob, then stepped back and allowed evolution to take over. It also accepts the stories of Genesis and most of the Bible as myths or fables. Of course, this means the Bible's picture of a concerned God involved in the lives of His people is incorrect.

Pantheistic Creation. Pantheism is the belief that God is in everything. God is a force inside all of us. In this belief, the divine consciousness in all of nature is the creator. The formation of the earth and the evolution of life on it occurred because the force inside made it happen.

Progressive Creation. This theory states that God created the earth and all life out of nothing during six vast periods of time. The six days of creation

in the Bible are seen as symbolic. The fossils in rocks are considered to be creatures that died out in ages gone by. This theory is in conflict with the biblical record of the origin of the seventh-day Sabbath, of sin, and of death.

Special Creation. This theory is the most straightforward interpretation of the first two chapters of Genesis. Here, God is presented as the Creator of both the nonliving and living matter in our solar system and the universe. The biblical record states that life and all life forms on this planet were created in six literal days, not six long periods of time. The supremacy of human beings is the result of being created "in the image of God" rather than evolving from lower primates.

Special creation is the only theory that follows the teaching of Scripture and fits the scientific evidence available. It allows for an involved, loving God and the assurance that what is in God's Word is true and is His message to us. Those who believe in special creation can have confidence that the history of the human race began in a perfect paradise with the Creator and that it will continue throughout eternity in a restored perfect paradise with a God whose love never ends.

Perhaps most important of all, special creation undergirds an understanding of the cross and our salvation. Christ's death on the cross speaks of God's great redeeming love for a race lost in sin. Evolution says that men and women, with no need of God, are good—and getting better all the time. If Jesus died on the cross for lost people, then evolution is a lie. If evolution is right, then believing in the cross is foolish.

EVOLUTION OR CREATION

If we analyze each of the proposed theories for the origin of life, we will discover that each requires some degree of faith. No single theory perfectly answers all the questions.

Evolution offers continuity to the human race only as long as human beings can change, evolve, and survive. Creation offers eternal life to each individual who believes in the Creator who was willing to die on a cross for His creation.

Evolution lifts humans up and makes "self" the most important and promotes survival and personal advancement at any price. Creation and the cross invite us to turn away from "self" and turn to God for happiness and eternal meaning.

With evolution, each person is a small, insignificant life form, destined to a short existence in a brutal world where individuals climb to the top by pushing others down, where the only happiness comes from grabbing all you can get.

With special creation, each person has value as the child of a loving God, destined to live forever in deepening relationships, where happiness comes from giving.

Which will you choose for yourself? ⚹

 Memory Focus

"By the word of the Lord the heavens were made, and all the host of them by the breath of His mouth. . . . For He spoke, and it was done; He commanded, and it stood fast" (Psalm 33:6, 9, NKJV).

. . . .

 Into the Bible

1. Read Psalm 33, and then answer the following questions by reading the verses noted.

   A. **Psalm 33:8, 9.** Why should the earth fear the Lord and stand in awe of Him?
   B. **Psalm 33:10-12.** How do God's plans compare with the plans of people?
   C. **Psalm 33:13-15.** What does God see as He looks down from heaven? What does He do?
   D. **Psalm 33:20-22.** Why is it good to wait on the Lord? What is the result of trusting God?

2. Read Nehemiah 9:5-12, and answer the following questions.

   A. What are the three reasons why the Lord should be praised and blessed?
   B. What four places does it say God created?
   C. What does God do for these four places and everything in them?

3. Read John 1:1-4, and answer the following questions.

   A. What four statements in these verses specifically teach against evolution?
   B. Why are these verses significant in refuting those who claim that the stories in Genesis are just fables?

4. Read 1 John 5:11-15, and answer the following questions.

    A. Who is the source of eternal life?

    B. How can you know you have eternal life? What kind of life do you think evolution has to offer?

 Projects

1. To appreciate the design and beauty of nature, we must observe it. Spend twenty to thirty minutes observing a living object (plant or animal). Notice carefully the evidences of a design. Write a summary of your observation.

2. Find the answer to the following questions in the narrative of this lesson.

    A. What is religious about the theory of evolution?

    B. What is scientific about creationism?

3. Find the answer to the following questions in the narrative of this lesson.

    A. What is the difference between theistic evolution and deistic evolution?

    B. What is the difference between progressive creation and special creation?

4. Find the answers to the following questions in the narrative of this lesson.

    A. Who would be the source of life for someone who believes in macroevolution?

    B. Who would be the source of life for someone who believes in pantheistic evolution?

    C. What kind of life does evolution have to offer?

 **Focus Questions**

1. Why is evolution called scientific?
2. Could you call evolution religion? Why or why not?
3. Should we be able to find scientific evidence to support the Bible story of Creation and the Flood? In your opinion, is there enough evidence?
4. How does theistic evolution limit God?
5. What does deistic evolution imply about God?
6. How does progressive creationism impact our understanding of the origin of sin and death in this world?
7. Is it easier to believe that this world was created by chance or by design?

UNDERCOVER

The atheist can't find God for the same reason that a thief can't find a police officer *(Quips and Quotes)*.

Creation: Fact or Fiction

Lesson Scriptures: Genesis 1; John 1:1-4; Isaiah 40:28-31; Isaiah 43:1

Blam! Like a Fourth of July firecracker cannon, the bus tire blew, and the science field trip took a sudden detour to the side of the road. With the bus parked precariously between the pavement and a canyon deep enough to disappear into, the teacher took advantage of an opportunity to make a point.

Gathering the students under the shade of the only tree in sight, he pointed to the canyon. "How long do you think it took that stream to carve this canyon?"

The students stared and blinked at the canyon walls and the tiny stream that wound its way along the bottom. A brave one ventured, "A long time?"

The teacher rolled his eyes. "I would guess, based on the rate of erosion by a stream of that size and the type of rock in this area that it has taken between five thousand and ten thousand years."

"Ooooh." The students were impressed.

As they talked, an old man in a pickup truck pulled slowly off the road and stopped beside the tree. "Trouble?" he asked.

"Just a flat tire," the teacher answered. "The bus driver will have it fixed quickly." Then a thought struck him. "Say, why don't you give us your opinion? How long do you think it took to form this canyon?"

The old man stared at the teacher.

"Just a rough guess—five, ten thousand years?"

"Nope."

"A thousand?" persisted the teacher.

"Nope."

The teacher frowned. "Then how long?"

"'Bout three days."

The teacher threw up his hands. "That's impossible," he exclaimed as he turned and walked toward the canyon.

One of the students spoke up. "Hey, he's a science teacher. Do you think you know more than he does about erosion and time?"

The old man shrugged. "Five years ago, that stream was in a gully 'bout half as deep as you are tall. Then an old earth dam upstream collapsed. I watched. In three days, the water and rocks cut this canyon down to where it is today."

"Ooooh."

The old man shifted into gear, then added. "I ain't arguing with your teacher. He's just got one problem with figurin' how long it took to cut this canyon. He didn't see it happen."

FACT OR FICTION

Is the story of Creation and the Flood fact or fiction? Many people today, even many Christians, consider the Creation story in the Bible a myth or a legend. They think the book of Genesis is a work of fiction, a made-up tale to inspire early believers. Why do special creationists believe it's true?

Special creationists accept the story of Creation in the Bible as it is written. Even though Moses was not there, God revealed the scenes of Creation to him. Through divine inspiration, Moses wrote in Genesis 1 to 3 what he was shown.

There is scientific evidence that the story in Genesis is true. The same evidence that evolutionists use to support their theory can be used to support special creationism.

A. Many animals have basically the same skeleton structure. And on the microscopic level, the cells of most life forms are very much alike. Evolutionists see this as evidence that all life is related, that it all evolved from the same parent cells.

Special creationists see this as evidence that life on this planet was designed. Life

forms and cells are similar because they were designed by an intelligent Creator.

B. Fossils are found throughout the rock layers that cover the earth. These layers are known as the geologic column. In this column, the older rock layers are those farthest down in the earth. Evolutionists say that fossils found in the layers progress from the more simple life forms at the lower levels to the more complex life forms at the higher levels. This is seen as evidence that the life forms evolved over the millions of years it took to lay down the rock formations.

Special creationists point out that the cells of the life forms preserved as fossils are complex even at the lowest levels. In fact, many of those simple life-form fossils are very much like creatures living today.

The more advanced life-form fossils found higher up in the rocks are evidence that the more intelligent, more mobile animals tried to escape the floodwaters and mud. They moved up to higher ground, just as you would expect.

As in our introduction story, evolutionists want to judge the earth's age by how long it would take today to form the rock layers that we see. Special creationists believe in catastrophism, that is, they believe that a major catastrophe laid down those rock layers far faster than is happening today. In the Flood, mass quantities of water and mud moved quickly. There is no way to compare that disaster with the normal movement of water and formation of rocks.

Another good evidence of the Flood, as mentioned in the last lesson, is turbidites—rock layers formed by rapidly moving underwater mud slides, just as you would expect to find after a worldwide flood and large rock formations that cover hundreds of thousands of square miles. Only a flood could lay out a layer of mud and debris over such a vast area.

C. Evolutionists claim that according to radiometric

dating, the earth is millions of years old. Radiometric dating is not a way to trick people. It is a scientifically correct way to measure how long certain radioactive elements in rocks have been releasing radiation. Scientists claim that it measures rocks and the fossils in them to be millions of years old.

Special creationists believe those measurements of millions of years could mean one of the following:

A. God created Adam a grown adult. In the same way, He created the earth as a mature planet where rocks appear millions of years old.

B. The Flood, and the forces that caused all that water to break loose and rearrange the face of the earth, disturbed and changed the normal radiation release patterns of those elements. This makes those readings incorrect.

C. The original rocks of this earth really are that old. Obviously, other parts of the universe existed before the earth did (heaven, as well as other places—Job 38:4-7; Hebrews 1:2, NIV). According to Genesis 1:1, 2, as Creation week began, something was already here. Verse 2 says that the Spirit of God moved over the water. Genesis 1 doesn't say that God created water or land. It says that He separated them.

Perhaps God created the foundations of this world when He created the rest of the universe, maybe millions of years ago. Then during the Creation week, He shaped it and filled it with life. This could

explain how the materials that formed the rock layers and the fossils in those rocks would seem to be millions of years old.

So there is evidence to believe in special creation. And that's important, because what you believe about Creation affects many other aspects of life.

If you are a deistic evolutionist and you believe God started the evolutionary process and left it to continue on its own, then you really believe that God is no longer involved with this world or its people.

If you are a theistic evolutionist and you believe that God created and has changed this world and its people by evolution, then you have to set aside large sections of the Bible as just stories and myths. If you do that, how do you know which parts are important? If Genesis is not true, what about Matthew? And would a loving God use the violence in evolution to accomplish His purpose?

If you are a progressive creationist and you believe that God created the world in six long geological time periods, then it really doesn't matter on which day you worship.

But if you are a special creationist and you believe in six real days of Creation, then a belief in the seventh-day Sabbath makes sense. This is the only belief about Creation that supports what the Bible teaches about the Sabbath or explains why it is an important occasion.

A belief about Creation is not just important in Genesis. In Revelation 14:6, 7, an angel calls for the people of earth to worship God because He is the Creator. In verse 12, God's people are described as those who keep His commandments, which includes the fourth commandment about the Sabbath. And that makes sense! Believing that God created just as the Bible says leads us to want to worship God just as the Bible teaches.

Our beliefs about Creation impact more than just Sabbath worship. Christians believe that Jesus came and died to save us, to redeem us from sin. But why would Jesus need to come and rescue an upward-evolving race? If humanity is getting better, evolving higher, then time—not a Saviour on a cross—is the answer.

The cross of Christ and the doctrine of Darwin stand in opposition. If Calvary is true,

evolution cannot be. If evolution is right, Calvary is foolish. The cross of Christ speaks of God's great redeeming love for a race lost in sin. Evolution says humans, quite apart from God, are good and getting better all the time.

The cross offers salvation through the blood of Christ; evolution offers it through time. The cross calls us to stoop low in humility; evolution calls us to claw higher in the survival of the fittest. Calvary invites us to turn **from** self **to** God; evolution proclaims self **as** god—as the highest rung in the evolutionary ladder ascending upward toward perfection of the species.

In the end, despite evolution's exalted view of humans, Christ alone offers us hope. Evolution delivers only despair—and death. In evolution, each of us is simply a bubble on the slime pond of time plus matter plus chance that rises up for a brief moment—then pops—and is forgotten in the flow of an impersonal universe itself destined for destruction. But "if any one is in Christ, he is a new Creation; the old has gone, the new has come" (2 Corinthians 5:17, NIV).

John 1:1-3 describes Jesus as the Word and tells us that all things were created by Him. Because Jesus created us, He is the One who could be our Redeemer.

You can see how important it is to believe the Bible account of Creation. It is the foundation on which the whole plan of salvation is built. According to the Bible, Jesus created us and set a plan in motion to save us from the penalty of sin—death. He Himself came and paid the penalty that we deserve so that we could claim the gift of eternal life that He deserved.

If we don't believe that He created us, how can we believe the rest of what He has revealed? If He didn't really create us as the Bible says, how can we be sure that He will save us as the Bible says?

Believing in the Genesis account of Creation is the anchor that holds down the rest of our faith in God. Without it, we are drifting in uncertainty.

Believing in Jesus as our Creator does another thing for us. It makes a difference in our belief about who we are. Everyone at some time feels worthless and unimportant and questions whether anyone really cares about them. If you believe that your ancestors, because of a chemical "accident," climbed out of a slime pit and swung in trees, you may spend your whole life wondering if you have any value.

But if you believe your ancestors were formed by the hand of God and that God's plan is to make you eternally happy, then you won't have the same doubts about your value.

Everyone has times when they feel worthless and unimportant and question whether anyone really cares about them. What a powerful antidote it is to read in God's Word that He created humankind and knows each one. He loves you personally. He treasures you so much. He was willing to die so that you could live forever in happiness.

The Genesis story of Creation was revealed to the author and contains just the essential facts. Knowing that the account of Creation is true, however, gives us an advantage for believing in Jesus as our Creator and Redeemer, in the seventh-day Sabbath, and in our value as God's children. ⋏

Memory Focus

 # Into the Bible

1. Isaiah 40:28-31 is a promise given by God the Creator. Read these verses, and answer these questions:

   A. What five things does it say about God?
   B. What will happen to those who trust (wait on) God?
   C. What difference does it make to the meaning of your life to know God is your Creator?

2. Another reason we can believe that the stories in the book of Genesis are true is that Jesus referred to them Himself. If those people and their lives were just myths, He would have spoken of them in a different way. Look up the following texts, and write down the phrases that refer to a reference in Genesis.

   A. Matthew 24:37
   B. John 8:58
   C. Luke 3:38
   D. Luke 13:28
   E. Matthew 19:4

3. Many Christians feel that the story of Creation is part of the Old Testament that is no longer important to Christians. Use the worksheet provided by your teacher to record, in your own words, New Testament teachings about Creation.

 # Projects

1. Divide the class into groups of four. Assign each group to prepare a classroom skit done as an on-the-spot TV report from one of the following:

   A. Report from the scene of Creation as described in Genesis. Report on what you see and hear. From your perspective, tell what the future offers for this new world and its life forms.

B. Report from the scene of evolution as the first life form crawls out of the slimy ocean. Report on what you see and hear, and tell what the future may hold for this new accident called life.

2. Write a newspaper article based on this headline: **HOW DID LIFE BEGIN? NEW THEORY SUGGESTS A MASTER DESIGN.** Write the article as if special creation were a new theory that no one had heard of. Include both scientific and scriptural evidence.

3. Knowing that God created us and redeemed us is a big boost to our concept of self-worth. He really cares! Read Psalm 139; then rewrite verses 1 to 6 and 13 to 16 in your own words. Think about the fact that God knows you better even than you know yourself—and He still loves you!

 Focus Questions

1. In the introductory story, what problem did the teacher have in common with scientists today?
2. Why can the same evidence used to support evolution be used to support creation?
3. As a creationist, how would you explain that simpler, smaller forms of life are found lower in the geologic column and larger, lower, more complex life forms are found higher up?
4. What is catastrophism, and how does it support the story of Creation and the Flood?
5. Which of the three possible answers to the millions of years of radiometric dating do you think best supports creationism?
6. How would being a theistic evolutionist affect other Christian beliefs?
7. How does believing in special creation affect what you think about yourself?

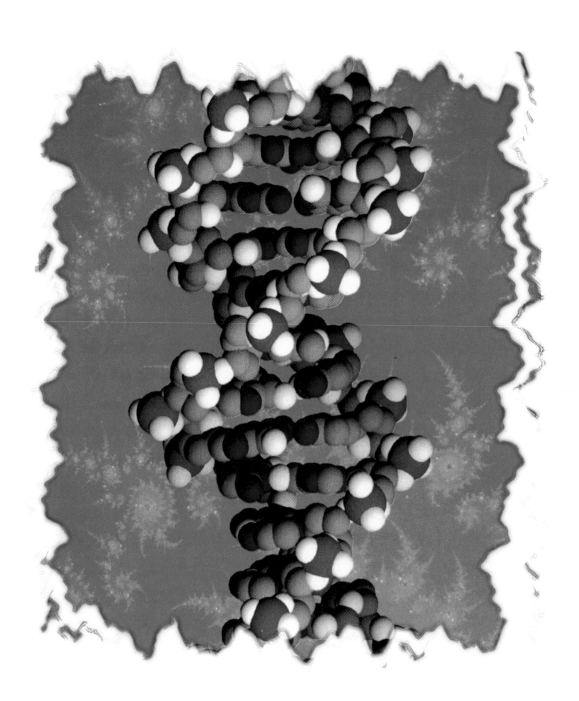

DESIGNER GENES

I praise you because I am fearfully and wonderfully made
(Psalm 139:13, 14, TLB).

lesson 11

The Gift of Creation

Lesson Scripture: Genesis 1, 2

The crowd of fifteen thousand pulled their coats tighter around their chests and stood silently in the Pennsylvania field. They craned their necks for a view of the podium and strained their ears for any word they could catch. The speaker had no microphone, but his voice carried well in the cold November air.

Just four months earlier, many of these same people had watched from sidelines as seven thousand men and boys died in this field outside the town of Gettysburg. Now they had come to dedicate a new cemetery on the site of one of the bloodiest battles of the Civil War.

Some came out of genuine respect. Many came out of curiosity—the President of the United States and many other dignitaries were on the platform that day. But most had come to hear Senator Edward Everett, one of the nation's most famous speakers. And on this occasion, the senator didn't let them down. For two straight hours, he transfixed the eager crowd with his flowery oratory and impassioned plea against the war. Finally, Everett sat down and, after a solemn hymn, Abraham Lincoln stood to say a few words of dedication.

He began with that now-famous phrase, "Fourscore and seven years ago, our fathers brought forth . . ." In what is now known as the Gettysburg Address, President Abraham Lincoln took only two minutes to honor those who died in battle and to inspire his listeners to defend the proposition that "all men are created equal." When Lincoln was finished, the long-winded senator said to him, "I should be glad if I could flatter myself that I came as near to the central idea of the occasion in two hours as you did in two minutes."

Fortunately, historians and speech teachers have agreed with Everett. Lincoln's short, profound speech has been engraved in stone, reprinted in countless textbooks, and memorized by millions of students. Everett's speech, on the other hand, is largely lost in the mists of history, proving once again that a few powerful words can say more than hours of empty oratory.

Lincoln was a diligent student of the Bible, and much of his writing and public speech mirrors the simple, powerful language of the prophets. Look at the very first chapter of Genesis. Here, Moses takes an astonishingly small number of words to describe an almost unimaginable event—the creation of the world. Moses must have sensed that when it came to describing the indescribable, a few well-chosen words are best. But even though his account is brief, it definitely has a pattern. Moses describes Creation in three stages: first the universe, then the earth, then the Garden of Eden. The entire first stage is covered in Genesis 1:1, where Moses says that God created "the heavens" as well as the earth. Don't bother to look for any details. When did God do it? How did He do it? How long did it take? We're not told. Moses seems in a hurry to get to the second stage—the creation of our world.

In verse 2, Moses writes that after God created it, the earth was "without form and void," which means it was unformed and unfilled. The story of Creation as given in Genesis is the account of how God formed the earth and filled it in seven days.

➤ **Days 1–3: God formed the earth.**

Day 1
He divided light from darkness (verses 3–5).

Day 2
He divided lower and upper waters (verses 6–8).

Day 3
He divided water from land (verses 9, 13).

In the next three days, He went back to fill what He had formed.

➤ **Days 4–6: God filled the earth.**

Day 4
He caused lights to appear in the sky (verses 14–19).

Day 5
He made creatures of the sea and air (verses 20–23).

Day 6
He made land animals and humans (verses 24–31).

➤ **Finally, on the seventh day, God finished His work by creating a time of rest and fellowship (Genesis 2:1-3).**

Moses tells us that God spoke the world into existence. He said, "Let there be light," and light appeared. But once again, the details are sketchy. Did God really use so few words? What language did He speak? How long did it take? Did the sky light up in a flash, as though God had thrown a master switch? Or did it begin as a tiny glow and fill the sky like a sunrise? Either Moses himself didn't know, or he didn't choose to tell us. But in any case, in just a few simple words, he drew a picture of Creation and the God who spoke it into being; that has captured imaginations for thousands of years.

The third stage of Creation is the most personal. God "planted a garden in Eden" as a home for the humans He had just created. But that gets us into another story that doesn't concern us here. Instead, let's skip ahead to Genesis 2:4-25, the second account of the Creation story. Here, Moses looks at the same events from a different angle. In Genesis 1, Moses introduces a God who is the Creator of life and Master of the universe. Here, he introduces a more personal God, one who cares about the beings He has created. Both accounts get at the heart of some of the most basic questions human beings can ask—questions we still ask ourselves today.

WHERE DID WE COME FROM?

Moses' description of how God created Adam, and then Eve, is one of the best-known stories in the world, perhaps because it shows God in a very personal, intimate light. He has just finished creating the universe and filling the earth by His word alone, perhaps from a very long way off. Who knows? But now He does something different. Picture Him on His hands and knees, forming a wet ball of mud into a magnificent man, "getting His hands dirty," so to speak. When He's breathed His own breath of life into Adam, He makes Adam His partner in the creation of Eve, putting him to sleep and taking a rib from his side. Then when man and woman are finished, God makes them a home.

WHY ARE WE HERE?

Eve and Adam were surrounded by joy, harmony, and abundant life. So what was the purpose of their lives? For one thing, there was a whole world to explore, and everything in it reminded them of God's love and how much they still had to learn about it. They were to take care of the earth and fill it with their children (Genesis 1:28). And being "newly born" themselves, God gave them the chance to grow and mature. He gave them freedom to choose and to develop their characters.

WHERE ARE WE GOING?

The Bible says that when God formed Adam from the dust, He "breathed into his nostrils the breath of life." This breath of life turned a clay mannequin into a living person, or "soul."

But what happens when the breath of life goes out? What happens to this soul when you die? There's a lot of confusion on this point. Many people believe that the soul is immortal, that it never dies but lives on in some other place or some other form. By this way of thinking, souls can return to haunt houses they once lived in or be reincarnated as another person or animal or become like angels and watch over us from heaven.

The Bible doesn't support any of these beliefs. The Bible teaches that death is an unconscious state in which the dead no longer exist and know nothing of what is happening in the world. The body returns to the dust it was made from, and the spark of life simply goes out.

Of course, this isn't the way God intended it to be. God gave Adam and Eve the tree of life.

They were welcome to eat the fruit of it, and as long as they did, they would never die. But this eternal life came with a condition—an unbroken relationship with God, the source of life. If they broke that relationship by doubting God's truthfulness or love, then their connection with life itself would be broken, and they would surely die. The lesson was clear.

Eternal life was not in the body or the soul. It was in a relationship with God.

The same God who spoke the world into being and made our ancestors out of dust offers eternal life to us. But the condition is the same. We can have a connection with the source of life that will continue for eternity, or we can choose death. It's up to us.

Memory Focus

"In the beginning God created the heavens and the earth" (Genesis 1:1, NIV).

OR

"This is the account of the heavens and the earth when they were created" (Genesis 2:4, NIV).

Into the Bible

1. Moses left out more details about Creation than he put in. As an exercise in creative writing, select any two days of Creation as recorded in Genesis 1:2–2:3, and fill in the details from your imagination. What would you have seen, heard, felt, and smelled if you had been a witness to Creation?
2. Compare Genesis 1 with John 1:1-4, 14, NIV. What does John add to the Creation story? Give the text and statement that

make reference to the participation of the Holy Spirit in Creation.

3. When you study Genesis 1 and 2, what are some things you can learn about God—His attributes, character, abilities?

4. Genesis records two accounts of Creation. Seven pairs of facts are given below. Write an example of each fact under the correct heading—**Genesis 1:2-31** or **Genesis 2:5-25.** Indicate the verse where the information is found or where it is emphasized. Use the worksheet provided by your teacher to record your answers.

   A. 1. God created the world.
      2. God planted a garden.
   B. 1. God created by speaking.
      2. God created by forming.
   C. 1. Focus is on the sixth day of Creation.
      2. Attention is given to each day of Creation.
   D. 1. God did the work of Creation.
      2. Adam was given work to do.
   E. 1. God created man before woman.
      2. God created humans.
   F. 1. Adam is warned about evil.
      2. Only good is created.
   G. 1. Humans were to subdue the earth.
      2. Marriage is given to humans.

5. *Stewardship* is a word we usually associate with money. But God intends people to be stewards, or managers, of everything He has given them.

   A. What did God give Adam and Eve to manage? Read Genesis 1:26-31 and Genesis 2:7-17 to find what these texts tell us about managing God's gifts.
   B. Identify ways in which this principle is violated in the world today.

6. Answer the following questions about immortality and death:

   A. How do we know that immortality was conditional for Eve and Adam? Genesis 2:17; 3:19.

B. What do the following texts say about death? Ecclesiastes 9:5, 10; Psalm 115:17; Psalm 146:4; John 5:28, 29.

C. When and how do we become immortal? 1 Corinthians 15:51-54.

 # Projects

1. What was the light God created on the first day of Creation? Use the *Index to the Writings of Ellen G. White,* Bible commentaries, and Bible dictionaries to write a paragraph explaining what that light might have been.
2. Read the article from the November 21, 1985, *Adventist Review* titled "Why (and how) was light created before the sun?" and write a one-paragraph reaction. (A copy of the article is available from your teacher.)
3. Identify what we can learn about healthful living from the Creation stories in Genesis 1 and 2.

 # Focus Questions

1. Why do you think there are two records of Creation, in Genesis 1 and Genesis 2?
2. Why do you think it is important that the first marriage is recorded in Scripture?
3. How did God provide for Eve and Adam to develop their characters?
4. In the world around you, can you see any consequences of the belief in an immortal soul?
5. Why did God give Adam and Eve the tree of the knowledge of good and evil?

HUMILITY

God has two thrones: One is in the highest heaven; the other is in the lowliest heart *(The Daily Walk)*.

Sabbath: A Day of Celebration

Lesson Scripture: Genesis 2:1-3

I have remained a Seventh-day Adventist today because of a "faith healing." You see, years ago I suffered from the Sundown Syndrome. This affliction strikes most Sabbath keepers at some time in their lives. It is especially lethal among teenagers and strikes particularly hard during Daylight Savings Time. The major symptom of this syndrome is a peaking of emotions in direct proportion to the setting sun on Saturday evening, reaching a critical stage as the sun sinks below the horizon, known as Saturday Night Fever.

The tragedy of the Sundown Syndrome, as those afflicted with it can tell you, is that "keeping" the Sabbath becomes associated with "doing time." This is how prisoners refer to their jail sentences. And sure enough, for the restless Sabbath keeper counting the boring hours until sundown, Sabbath is a jail, God is the warden, and you just can't wait to break out.

Boredom may not sound like such a serious affliction to you—surely not bad enough to require a faith healing. But as a young man, my frustration with Sabbath keeping got so serious that I was in danger of losing my life-giving relationship with God. I either had to find new ways to make the Sabbath a celebration instead of a sentence, or I knew I would end up rejecting the beliefs I was raised by. Then I remembered that God had said, "Taste and see that the Lord is good" (Psalm 34:8). So I decided to run a taste

test. I prayed, "Lord, show me how to make the Sabbath a delight. Heal me from the Sundown Syndrome."

The healing didn't take place immediately. It was more like a journey that, for me, began with a new look at the Bible. Having gone to church school for years, I thought I knew everything about the Sabbath that I would ever need to know. But I discovered that while I knew how to use texts to *prove* the Sabbath, I didn't know the first thing about how to *live* the Sabbath. So I took a concordance and looked up all the passages that referred to Sabbath. Of course, that took me all the way back to Genesis.

As I studied the account of Creation week, I began to see *one important difference between the way I was keeping the Sabbath and the way God created it*: God had a plan, and I didn't. "Planning" my Sabbath-afternoon activities usually involved going to Sabbath School and seeing what everybody else was doing. Of course, they had all made the same "plan," which is why so many Sabbaths were spent just driving around or sleeping all afternoon.

But God doesn't work like that. He has had a plan for us "from the foundation of the world." You can see that foresight unfolding in the story of creation and redemption. In the first six days of creation, God provided lavishly for our physical needs. But He knew we were not merely creatures. He had given us "living souls" that thrive on love and relationships. So He created a day that would provide us with everything we need to be fully alive. I started to think of it this way: In six days God provided for life, and on the seventh day, He provided for love.

How did God provide for love? As I found more verses about the Sabbath, I saw that there were three basic elements built right into this special day: (1) rest, (2) blessing, and (3) sanctification (a big word for a fairly simple idea that we will discuss later). Let's look at them one at a time.

REST

Before my faith healing, my concept of Sabbath rest was fairly limited. Basically, it boiled down to a list of things I didn't do on Sabbath, plus taking a long nap. Slowly I began to see that inactivity was just a small

part of the rest God had in mind.

Maybe a good place to begin is to think about the opposite of rest. For most of us, it is stress. Many of us are stressed out. Our lives are full of hard work, high expectations, and the hurt that comes from trying and failing. If rest means anything, surely it means a break from *that*. So Sabbath is God's stress buster, a time out of the week to stop and renew the sense that everything will be all right because God is in charge of our lives. The more stressful and anxious we are, the more we need Sabbath.

But how do we get that feeling? How do we unwind at the end of a busy and disappointing week and let God fill us with His love? Well, to experience anyone's love, you have to feel secure in their presence, and it's the same with God. You can relax and be yourself, knowing that you are accepted as you are and that no matter what happens, He will go through it with you.

BLESSING

The second element I discovered was blessing. This, too, has come to mean some-

thing quite limited, such as saying grace before a meal. But there's so much more to it than that. When you ask for someone's blessing, you are asking for their approval. To really feel good about ourselves, we all need approval from the people who matter most to us, especially our parents. Each of us spends a good deal of our childhood trying to get our

parents' blessing on our activities, our friends, even our hairstyles. And sometimes it's pretty hard to come by. Maybe that's why we have a hard time understanding the concept of God's blessing.

Sadly, far too many of us grow up without the approval we need from our parents. Some parents are abusive, sending the message in a hundred different ways that "you're no good." Other parents are indifferent, and that can be just as bad. Instead of listening and getting involved, they hand their kids some money and say, "Here, have some fun. Just get outta here."

Some parents think they're doing their duty by setting impossibly high standards. If you get a B+, they ask why you didn't get an A-. If you hit a double, they say, "You could have had a triple if you'd tried harder." They may mean well, but you're left with the feeling that you just don't measure up, no matter how hard you try.

For each of these hurting people, God wants to be the perfect parent. Every Sabbath, He sends the message that He thinks you are special.

You have value and tremendous worth in His eyes. Every Sabbath He is saying, "You mean a great deal to Me. I have redeemed you by My own blood. You are My child, and I have given you everything." When we slow down on Sabbath and take time to sense God's approval, we receive the Sabbath blessing He intended.

SANCTIFICATION

Here's that big word again. But let's tame it with a little definition. *To sanctify* literally means "to set apart for a special purpose." So what is God's special purpose for us, and how does the Sabbath help fulfill that promise?

When Jesus spoke directly to His disciples about why He had chosen them and set them apart as special, He said, "A new commandment I give unto you that you love one another. By this all men will know that you are my disciples" (John 13:34). He knew that community, or coming together, was so important and so rare in this world that it would be the most convincing evidence of the power of God's love.

People have a strong need to be part of a community. They form neighborhood associations, they join clubs, they go to concerts or sporting events to be with people like themselves. But a community of Christians is unique, because we not only share a common interest; we share a common love. We know that God has chosen us, and we've allowed Him to change us from people who fight and bicker and blame into people who love, forgive, and grow together. Sabbath is a time when we get right with each other in preparation for being right with God. It brings us together in a community of love and sets us apart for our work as God's disciples on earth.

That's the basic outline of my "faith healing," a journey through the Bible that gave the Sabbath new meaning for me. The best news I discovered was that the Sabbath was made for people and not the other way around (Mark 2:27). When Jesus came, the day He had created for rest, blessing, and sanctification had become a day of restrictions, rules, and regulations. He sought to restore His original intent. He intended Sabbath to be a time for nurturing a relationship between Himself and His creatures. The Sabbath was made for us, to provide us with the most important element in life—love. ⚰

Memory Focus

"Then he said to them, "The Sabbath was made for man, not man for the Sabbath" (Mark 2:27, NIV).

OR

"Come to me, all you who are weary and burdened, and I will give you rest" (Matthew 11:28, NIV).

 # Into the Bible

1. Read Genesis 2:1-3. What elements, or principles, did God build into the Sabbath?
2. Read the following texts. Identify the additional meanings to the word *rest* as found in each: Matthew 11:28; Joshua 1:13; Hebrews 4:8-10.
3. Read the following texts, and define the various concepts of blessings: Nehemiah 8:8-10; Psalm 118:24; 1 John 3:1; Genesis 12:2; 28:10-17; 48:3, 9-16. Which of these texts outlines the steps involved in giving a biblical blessing?
4. Read these texts on the subject of sanctification, and state in a few words what each suggests sanctification is: Hebrews 10:10; Colossians 1:27; 1 Thessalonians 5:23; Joshua 3:5; Isaiah 1:16-18.
5. Compare the reasons why God asks us to keep the Sabbath holy in Exodus 20 with the one in Deuteronomy 5.

 # Projects

1. Write four personal Sabbath Celebration plans using the Sabbath Planning Worksheet supplied by your teacher.

2. Create a short drama that portrays God's purpose in creating the Sabbath.
3. Join a group that plans, implements, and evaluates a Sabbath Celebration for your youth group (academy, Sabbath School) using the Sabbath Planning Worksheet.
4. Plan and live a Sabbath that demonstrates how you think Jesus would keep Sabbath if He came to our world today.
5. Study the healing miracles Jesus performed on Sabbath. Read Matthew 11:28–12:4; Matthew 12:9-15; Luke 6:6-10; Luke 13:10-16; Luke 14:1-6; John 5:1-9; John 9:1-14. Which of the three Sabbath principles of rest, blessing, and sanctification does each fulfill?

 **Focus Questions**

1. How has the "Sabbath Syndrome" affected you or your family?
2. Genuine Sabbath observance helps one grow to be more like Jesus. Why?
3. Why is the realization of God's acceptance of you through Christ important to genuine Sabbath rest?
4. This lesson challenges us to take the "taste test." Is Christianity true because it works? Explain your answer.

BALANCE

Freedom is a package deal—it comes with responsibilities and with consequences (Gordon Kainer).

Rebellion: The Lucifer Scenario

Lesson Scripture: Isaiah 14:12-14

When you think of Satan, what do you see in your mind's eye? An impish sort of fellow in a red jumpsuit, complete with tail, horns, and pitchfork? Probably not. What, then? A hideous, monsterlike creature? A brute beast from your worst nightmare? If outward appearance always reflected inner character, I would say you were getting warmer. But the truth is, evil sometimes comes wrapped in a pretty package, delivered with a charming smile.

So if being evil or satanic doesn't necessarily mean being gross and monstrous, what does it mean? What is evil? What turned Lucifer, Son of the Morning, into Satan? What turned an angel into a demon who infected the earth with deception, disease, and death?

That's a lot of questions to start off with. But the answers can all be found in the books of the prophets, especially Isaiah and Ezekiel. Both prophets denounce wicked human kings, then reveal that the real power behind these rulers is Satan. Let's look first at what Isaiah says about how Lucifer became Satan:

"How you have fallen from heaven,
O morning star, son of the dawn!
You have been cast down to the earth,
You who once laid low the nations!
You said in your heart,
'I will ascend to heaven;

I will raise my throne above the stars of God;

I will sit enthroned on the mount of assembly,

on the utmost heights of the sacred mountain.

I will ascend above the tops of the clouds;

I will make myself like the Most High.'

But you are brought down to the grave,

to the depths of the pit" (Isaiah 14:12-14, NIV).

If we look at these verses carefully, we can analyze Lucifer's original sin. It wasn't murder, sorcery, sex, drinking, or drugs. It wasn't physical action at all. It was a decision, a choice, an attitude about himself. If you're not convinced, count how many times the word *I* appears in the verses above. Lucifer had an "I" problem. His vision turned inward upon himself until he became the center of his universe. His transformation into Satan began when he made himself his own highest authority and the ruler of his own life, instead of putting his trust in God.

Lucifer's rebellion was remarkably subtle (something Adam and Eve regrettably discovered too late). He didn't

come right out and say, "I want to be gross, evil, and immoral! I want to be as different from God as I possibly can be." No, what he said was really just the opposite: "I want to be like God. I will make **myself** like the Most High."

The problem was that Lucifer didn't want to pattern his character on God's perfect goodness. He didn't want to be like God, something all Christians are taught to strive for. Lucifer wasn't motivated by a desire for holiness; he was jealous! *He* wanted to be the highest authority. *He* wanted to be worshiped. *He* wanted to be all-powerful. He wanted to run the universe *his* way, by his own rules. When he imagined the universe run according to his plan, God's plan seemed too restrictive. Unfortunately, Lucifer later learned that the smallest package in the universe is a creature wrapped up in himself.

A second description of Lucifer's rebellion is found in Ezekiel 28. The first ten verses are about the king of Tyre, a brutal, arrogant tyrant. But beginning with verse 11, the prophet says that the roots of this king's wickedness go all the way back to the first sin. Speak-

ing of Lucifer, Ezekiel says, "Your heart became proud on account of your beauty, and you corrupted your wisdom because of your splendor" (Ezekiel 28:17, NIV).

God had given Lucifer great and powerful gifts to use as a friend and servant to all. But Lucifer became obsessed with these gifts and how they could be used to enhance his own prestige. He tried to put himself above God by accusing Him of being arbitrary and untrustworthy. This led to war in heaven, and Lucifer was cast down.

THE LIE

This focus on self as "god" can be called the Lucifer scenario. It's at the heart of Lucifer's rebellion, and it's the disease that has since infected the whole human race. It's the lie Satan tries to get us to accept, until we "consent to live for the service of self, and Satan is satisfied" (*The Desire of Ages*, 130). Jesus even had to rebuke His disciple Peter for buying into this attitude. When Peter tried to prevent Jesus from going to His death, Jesus said, "Out of my sight, Satan! You are a stumbling block to me; you do not have in mind the things of God, but the things of men"

(Matthew 16:23, NIV).

How did Lucifer get away with it? Why didn't God stop him? Better yet, if God knows everything and knew Lucifer would rebel, why did He create him in the first place? Is God responsible for evil because He let Lucifer rebel?

THE TRUTH

The truth is that God was not arbitrary and untrustworthy, as Lucifer had implied. Quite the opposite. He refused to create beings who automatically did His will. The Bible is clear about how evil began. God did not create evil. But He did create beings who had freedom of choice—a freedom God refused to take away.

Satan wants to control us and hold us in bondage, even though he promises freedom. But God gave us true freedom, even though He knew that some would use their freedom to reject Him. He knows that only creatures who are truly free can truly love, and love is the essence of God. We can become "like God," not by focusing on ourselves, but on unselfish love to others. When we begin to love as God loves, we begin to be like God.

THE TEST

Evil exists as a parasite, attached to good. It destroys everything it infects. It distorts and twists God's gifts and uses them for self-gratification. It turns love into lust, pleasure into addiction, appetite into gluttony, need into greed. Remember, Lucifer was a created being. The remnants of the power God originally gave him is the only power he has. He has to rely on deceit to conquer human beings.

God gave Adam and Eve everything in the garden—everything except one tree. The tree of the knowledge of good and evil was good, beautiful, and fruitful. But it was also a test, an opportunity to exercise freedom of choice. To eat from it was to distrust God, deny His authority, and defy His will. It would be an act of open rebellion and a choice of death over life. It would be choosing to accept the Lucifer scenario. But God decided it was a choice Adam and Eve had to make for themselves. ⚘

Memory Focus

"Ye shall know the truth, and the truth shall make you free" (John 8:32, KJV).

OR

"So if the Son sets you free, you will be free, indeed" (John 8:36, NIV).

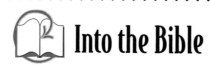

Into the Bible

1. Read Luke 18:9-14 and Revelation 3:14-19. According to these two passages, what are Jesus' serious concerns about people convinced of their own religious superiority and goodness? Which is worse, having pride about how bad you are or having pride about how good you are? Why?

2. Read Romans 13:8-10, and compare the text with Exodus 20:
   1-17. Explain how the Ten Commandments, when stated in a
   positive way, are a fulfillment of unselfish love.
3. Read the following texts, and identify what each teaches about
   "freedom in Christ."
   A. Revelation 1:5 (NIV)
   B. John 8:32-36 (NIV)
   C. Galatians 5:1, 13 (NIV)

 # Projects

1. Read *Patriarchs and Prophets,* pages. 33-43. Write a short summary of
   how and why jealousy pushed Lucifer's pride into open rebellion.
2. What does Jesus' death on the cross indicate about the worth
   of each person? What is the difference between having a positive feeling of self-worth and thinking of yourself as better and
   more deserving than others?
3. Ask two or three adults whom you trust to share their thinking
   on the questions in Project 2 with you, and write your findings
   in a few paragraphs.

Focus Questions

1. Most self-centered people don't go around saying, "I am god!"
   They have more subtle ways of making themselves the center of
   everything. What are some of these subtle techniques for
   making everything revolve around oneself?
2. Why is it important to God that we all have the freedom to
   follow Him or reject Him?
3. What are some of the behaviors, attitudes, and habits that
   enslave people in our society?
4. What does Jesus' death on the cross teach us about the following:
   A. Each person is of great worth or worthless.
   B. Each person is worthy or unworthy of salvation.

IS THE PRICE RIGHT?

Sin wouldn't be so attractive if the wages were paid immediately
(Quips and Quotes).

lesson 14

Sin: Seductive and Destructive

Lesson Scripture: Genesis 3:1-21 (NIV)

ave you ever noticed that in fictional movies or books the bad guys are almost always more interesting than the good guys? We may cheer for the good guy to win out in the end, but in the meantime, that clean-cut, upright, square-jawed fellow in the white hat is just a little, well, boring!

You're not the only one who's noticed that. Years ago, a young poet named Simone Weil fought against the Nazis in the French underground during World War II. Later, after she became a Christian, she wrote about a puzzling truth she had discovered:

"[In reality] nothing is so beautiful, nothing is so continually fresh and surprising, so full of sweet and perpetual ecstasy, as that which is *good;* while no desert is so dreary, monotonous and boring as *evil.* But with *fantasy* it's the other way around. *Fictional good* is boring and flat, while *fictional evil* is varied, intriguing, attractive and full of charm."[1] (Emphasis supplied.)

Weil makes an important distinction between fantasy and reality—a distinction we should keep in mind as we discuss the beginnings of sin in this lesson. For even Adam and Eve ran up against the troubling fact that evil is usually more attractive as a fantasy than as a reality.

---

[1] Quoted in Malcolm Muggeridge, *Christ and the Media* (Eerdmans, 1977), 46.

THE FIRST MARRIAGE

Soon after God created Adam, He gave Adam two things that would change his life forever. First, God gave Adam the tree of the knowledge of good and evil as a test of his loyalty and trust. God warned Adam, "In the day you eat of it you shall surely die." Second, for the sake of helping make their obedience joyful, God created a love relationship. He declared, "It is not good for the man to be alone; I will make for him a helper suitable for him" (Genesis 2:18, NIV).

So God created a woman, Eve, to be Adam's partner. Adam must have been thrilled when he awoke to find this lovely creature, as marvelous as himself, yet different from him in equally glorious ways. He undoubtedly shared God's opinion that she was "very good." (Read the full story in Genesis 2:19-25.)

THE FIRST DOUBT

It's hard for us now to imagine the perfection of this first marriage. This was what God intended for human relationships—a loving, sharing partnership. Eve's and Adam's love for each other and their love for God were all bound up together in joy, tenderness, and trust.

Imagining this perfect existence makes Satan's deception of these two seem all the more cunning and cruel. When he saw that the time was right, he took possession of a serpent and went into the garden to take possession of the minds and bodies of the first married couple.

Lounging on a branch of the tree of the knowledge of good and evil, the serpent struck up an innocent-sounding conversation with Eve. "Indeed, has God said, 'You shall not eat from any tree of the garden?'" (Genesis 3:1, NASB). Satan's question implied that perhaps God had been unreasonable, and it opened the door for other questions: Has God given you real freedom? Is He keeping you from enjoying life fully? Is He holding something back from you—something you would really like? He wanted Eve to consider that perhaps God could not be trusted.

Eve answered the serpent by repeating God's instructions in her own words:

"From the fruit of the trees

of the garden we may eat; but from the fruit of the tree which is in the middle of the garden, God has said, 'You shall not eat from it or touch it, lest you die'" (Genesis 3:2, 3, NASB).

Satan must have detected a hint of irritation or amazement in Eve's tone as she thought about God holding something back from her. Maybe it was the additional words "or touch it," as though she were saying, "Not *eat* it? Would you believe He won't even let us *touch* it without destroying us!" In any case, he must have thought it was time to move on to the next step.

Eve's little trace of doubt was just an opening. She was toying with the idea that maybe she didn't really need so many restrictions on her freedom. Now was the time to introduce some outright lies—three basic lies that are still the foundation of Satan's campaign against God's creation.

LIE #1
SIN WON'T HURT YOU

As soon as Eve declared that if she ate the fruit she would die, Satan countered with a startling but soothing assurance: "Don't believe it! You won't die." In this dramatic scene in the garden, God and Satan were surely battling for Eve's mind. But Satan had one clear advantage in this struggle—he could trick Eve through lies. God limits Himself to the truth, but Satan knows he can't afford that limitation. He knows the real, ugly consequences of sin, so he deals in fantasy. He promises things he knows he can never deliver.

Satan assured Eve that disobedience was not fatal, that sin had no serious consequences. "It's an empty threat, Eve. Go ahead. Enjoy!" He said she could do whatever she wanted and still be immortal. He promised what only God can deliver—eternal life.

LIE #2
SIN WILL ENHANCE YOUR LIFE

Satan moved from a negative lie, "You will not die," to a positive one, "You will be like God." He told Eve that striking out on her own would make her life more satisfying and exciting. "For God knows that in the day you eat from it your eyes will be opened, and you will be like God, knowing good and evil" (Genesis 3:5, NASB).

He promised deeper wisdom ("your eyes will be opened") and greater power and freedom ("you will be like God"). He invited Eve to see herself as divine, to put herself in the center of her universe, to be her own god. He promised that she could be the independent, all-wise ruler of her own life and not give up a thing—not even eternal life. "Do your own thing, Eve. Look out for yourself, and don't let God get in the way of your rights." It's been Satan's standard line to men and women ever since.

LIE #3
YOU CAN HAVE WHATEVER MAKES YOU FEEL GOOD— RIGHT NOW

Eve's head must have been reeling. Just imagine! To be the master of her own life. To make her own rules. And if she messed up? No big deal! There would be no serious consequences, no death penalty after all. What an intoxicating hook to dangle in front of Eve. But what was the bait? How did Satan finally get her to swallow this fantasy?

"When the woman saw that the tree was good for food, and that it was a delight to the eyes, and that the tree was desirable to make one wise, she took from its fruit and ate: and she gave also to her husband with her and he ate" (Genesis 3:6, NASB).

What Satan held out to her was a pleasurable experience that she could have right now, instead of waiting for some other pleasure that might or might not come farther down the road. God had promised to reward a lifetime of obedience with glories she couldn't even imagine. But here was this lovely fruit right here, right now. And it must have been a real delight to the senses—smell, touch, taste—which are, after all, the way we experience any pleasure. What a dilemma for Eve. Of course, we all know that she went ahead and picked the fruit and ate it. She started down that road as soon as she began to care more about what she was feeling than what God had said.

In giving in to temptation, Eve, and then Adam, forgot two very important truths. First, God is the inventor and giver of every real pleasure. We often forget that God isn't just a lawgiver. He's the creator of our senses and of all the positive things that give them pleasure.

Satan doesn't have God's creative power because he is not God's equal. He can't create new pleasures. He can only take a positive pleasure and pervert it, making it work against us. He can only turn eating into bulimia, drinking into drunkenness, sensuality into pornography.

Second, Eve and Adam forgot that sometimes we must give up one pleasure now so that we can have greater pleasure later. Children don't understand this. They always demand immediate gratification of their wishes. "I want new skates, and I want them *now!*" But a part of maturity is accepting what psychologists call "deferred gratification." It means putting off something good so that you can work for something even better. It means staying home and studying, even though you'd really rather go out with your friends, because you know that while going out with your friends is fun, in the long run, passing grades are going to do you more good. There are examples of deferred gratification all around you. College graduates, successful athletes, happily married couples, all know that discipline and commitment open the door to the most lasting pleasures and the greatest freedom.

WHAT SIN DELIVERED

"Each one is tempted when he is carried away and enticed by his own lust. Then when lust has conceived, it gives birth to sin; and when sin is accomplished, it brings forth death" (James 1:14, 15, NASB).

The rosy scenario Satan laid out for Adam and Eve was all based on lies. He said that like a willful little child, if they just yanked their hands out of God's and ran off on their own, they would be wiser, happier, and freer. But even a child who breaks free and runs away from his mother in a crowded department store finds out it's not such a good idea.

The outcome of that first sin has been that we've all lost our way. Instead of what Satan promised, we now live in a world filled with fear, shame, insecurity, loneliness, and death. Satan did deliver on one of his promises, though. Humans already understood God's goodness; now. they gained a knowledge of evil, but at a price none of us *could have imagined.* ⅄

 **Memory Focus**

"For the wages of sin is death, but the gift of God is eternal life in Christ Jesus our Lord" (Romans 6:23, NIV).

. . . .

 **Into the Bible**

1. Read Revelation 12:9 and 2 Corinthians 11:3. What do these verses have to say regarding Satan's use of the serpent as the medium for leading Eve into sin and what his real intent was?
2. Read Genesis 3:7-19. Identify verses that show that sin resulted in the following attitudes, emotions, and experiences.
   A. fear
   B. shame (guilt and regret)
   C. insecurity
   D. inability to be open and honest ("hid themselves")
   E. loss of intimacy with God and with each other
   F. blame (accusations)
   G. death
3. Going farther in the book of Genesis, read the following passages, and list additional long-term consequences of sin:
   A. Genesis 4:8, 9, 23, 24
   B. Genesis 6:5
   C. Genesis 11:4
   D. Genesis 27:1-41

. . . .

 **Projects**

1. Locate advertisements in news magazines that, through words, pictures, or both, promise something they can't deliver. Evalu-

ate what the ads promise, such as pleasure, beauty, popularity, and what they might actually deliver, such as disease, vanity, needless expense.

2. In the same news magazines used in project 1, locate news stories that deal with urban decay, ethnic strife, domestic violence, business upheavals, etc. Identify the basic human problems that lead to such conditions.

3. Find an article on "New Age" beliefs. Compare the key ideas of New Age thinking with what Satan promised Eve in the garden. See Genesis 3:4-6.

 # Focus Questions

1. What kind of attractive packaging does evil wear today to hide its true nature?
2. Think of some television programs or characters that illustrate the notion that, in fiction, at least, evil is fascinating and good is dull.
3. Why did Eve actually sin?
4. Throughout the Bible and in history, sin always wrecks close relationships and intimacy. Why do you think that happens? What is it about sin that damages or destroys relationships?
5. What is the difference between a "need" and a "want"? Which does advertising appeal to?

INVISIBLE

Above all, love each other deeply, because love covers over a multitude of sins (1 Peter 4:8, NIV).

God's Response to Sin

Lesson Scripture: Genesis 3:1-24

 **HE BAD NEWS AND THE GOOD NEWS**

Adam and Eve opened the way for sin to infect humanity. And the infection is 100 percent fatal. That is the **bad news** of Genesis 3.

The **good news** of Genesis 3 is the way God responded. When Adam and Eve disbelieved, disobeyed, and did their best to disappear, God responded in four ways.

1. God Took the Initiative.

God's **first response** was to lovingly seek Adam. He took the initiative. "The Lord God called to the man, 'Where are you?' " (Genesis 3:9, NIV). When Adam and Eve sinned, they tried to run and hide. When Adam and

Eve sinned, they did their best to cover up their guilt and shame, to make themselves look good. But God didn't wait for them to realize how hopeless they were. He didn't stand back, demanding that they first get good enough, and then maybe He'd talk to them again. God took the first step. He still does. He sought out the guilty couple to offer them more than just trying to look good. Though we didn't deserve His acceptance, and before we even knew how much we needed it, God reached out to us in love. Jesus didn't come just to help the good get better. He came to seek and save the lost (Luke 19:10).

2. God Promised a Saviour.

God's **second response** to sin is found in the very first

prophecy of Christ in the Bible (Genesis 3:15). God spoke this prophecy to the serpent (Satan, Revelation 12:9). God promised the human race a Saviour, who by His suffering would remove our sin, defang the serpent, and destroy death.

From the moment there was sin, there was a Saviour. God never expected or required us to save ourselves, because we can't. Our part in salvation is to recognize our need and come—just as we are—with all our problems and struggles to Jesus as Lord and Saviour.

3. God Told the Truth About Sin.

God's **third response** is found in Genesis 3:16-19, 23, 24. Read this passage, which is called the "Adamic Curse" (the curse on Adam and his children because of sin). In these few verses, God revealed what sin's true consequences would be for the human family. Notice the key words in these verses:

A. "In **pain** you shall bring forth children" (3:16).

B. "**Cursed** is the ground because of you" (3:17).

C. "In **toil** you shall eat of it" (3:17).

D. "Both **thorns and thistles** it shall grow for you" (3:18).

E. "By the **sweat** of your face . . ." (3:19).

F. "So he drove the man out [**separation**] . . . to guard the way to the tree of life" (3:23, 24).

G. "To dust you will return [**death**]" (3:19).

Seven terrible consequences of sin: pain, curse, toil, thorns and thistles, agonizing sweat, separation, and finally death. This is our inheritance from the first Adam, the sure consequences of sin.

There is only one other story in the Bible that specifically mentions these seven things—the story of Christ's crucifixion. They are found in the story of the cross because God did more than pronounce the curse; He also determined to remove it. Jesus came as the second Adam (Romans 5:12-19). At Calvary, He took the curse of Adam's sin upon Himself—and took it away!

Jesus came as the "Lamb of God that takes away the sin of the world" (John 1:29). Note

how Jesus experienced each of the seven consequences:

A. **pain:** Matthew 26:67; 27:26-31.

B. the **curse:** Mark 15:29-37; Galatians 3:13.

C. **toil:** Matthew 27:27-34.

D. **thorns and thistles:** John 19:2, 3.

E. **sweat**—"great drops of blood": Luke 22:42-44.

F. **separation:** Mark 15:33-38; Isaiah 53:4-6,10.

G. **death:** Matthew 27:46, 50, 51; Hebrews 2:9.

In Eden, God described what the consequences of sin would be for humanity. He told the truth. He revealed sin's devastating effects. But God did more than that. For every sinner who turns to Christ in trust and allegiance, God removes the curse that was placed on Adam.

4. God Provided a Substitute.

God's **fourth response** to sin in the garden was to provide the covering for Adam and Eve's nakedness (guilt and shame) through the shedding of blood—by a sacrifice (Genesis 3:21).

This sacrifice pointed to the true **substitute**, a word which means one who takes another's place (1 Peter 3:18). In basketball, when the buzzer sounds and a member of the team comes onto the court to replace another player, he is called a substitute. If the substitute

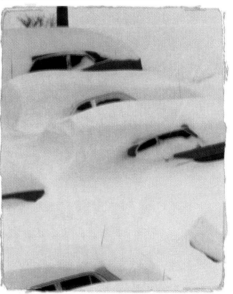

scores thirty points and wins the game, the whole team wins. The good news (gospel) is that whatever the substitute does, he not only does in place of his teammate, but for his teammate—indeed, for the whole team. If the substitute scores the winning basket, his whole team wins. His actions affect the standing of everyone on the team.

We are all guilty before God. We've lost the game! But by faith alone we can accept in our place the one-on-one victory of Jesus over sin. He achieved what we have failed to achieve (a sinless life) and yet received what each of us deserves (a sinner's death). Jesus took our place in judgment. He gave Himself as our substitute sacrifice and sin offering so that we might be covered with His righteousness.

Remember, Adam and Eve really were guilty of breaking God's command. Their sin was inexcusable in light of God's love and terrible in terms of the suffering it would bring upon the entire race. They deserved the final death God had warned sin would bring (Genesis 2:17). "The wages of sin is death" (Romans 6:23, NIV).

But Father and Son had made a choice that went into effect the moment Adam and Eve chose to sin. The very last book of the Bible describes God's choice to bear the sins of the world in Christ, "**the Lamb slain from the foundation of the world**" (Revelation 13:8, NIV).

The heart of the gospel is Jesus' death in our place for our sins as our substitute. The cross of Christ is God's ultimate response to sin.

"Christ was treated as we deserve, that we might be treated as He deserves. He was condemned for our sins, in which He had no share, that we might be justified by His righteousness, in which we had no share. He suffered the death which was ours, that we might receive the life which was His. 'With His stripes we are healed'" (*The Desire of Ages*, 25).

Memory Focus

"I will put enmity between you and the woman, and between your offspring and hers; he will crush your head, and you will strike his heel" (Genesis 3:15, NIV).

OR

"We all, like sheep, have gone astray, each of us has turned to his own way; and the Lord has laid on him the iniquity of us all" (Isaiah 53:6, NIV).

. . . .

Into the Bible

1. On a worksheet your teacher will provide, show the contrast between Adam and Christ.
2. Use the worksheet your teacher will provide to see how God knows our needs before we even seek Him.
3. Genesis 3:15 is the very first prophecy of Christ in the Bible. It centers on the conflict between the serpent and the "seed," or offspring, of the woman. Answer the following questions:

   A. According to Revelation 12:9 and 20:2, who is the serpent?
   B. Eve is the first woman, the bride of Adam. She was created in the image of God, fell into sin, and was redeemed by Christ. In the following verses, identify various ways the people of God (church) are compared to a woman: Hosea 2:14-16, 19, 20; 2 Corinthians 11:2, 3; Ephesians 5:23-32; Revelation 12:1-6.
   C. The word *seed* is singular in Genesis 3:15. In the original language, who does the seed represent? See Galatians 3:16 and Hebrews 2:9.
   D. How is the serpent's head "crushed" (Genesis 3:15, NIV)? See John 12:31; Hebrews 2:14; and Revelation 12:10, 11.

4. There are some who believe that it was not necessary for Jesus to die for our sins. Select key phrases from the following four verses that show what Jesus accomplished by His death.

   A. 2 Corinthians 5:21
   B. Romans 5:8
   C. 1 Peter 2:24
   D. 1 Peter 3:18

· ·

 # Projects

1. Divide the class into groups of four to six. Each group should:

   A. Make a list of four or five common coverups we are tempted to use when we have wronged or hurt someone.
   B. After the list is made, each group should discuss whether these common coverups really heal us or help the situation. Each group should appoint a spokesperson to summarize the group's discussion for the class.
   C. Each group should try to come to a common agreement on what Genesis 3:21 says about how God heals our sins and helps restore our relationship with Him.

2. The Bible does not teach that humans are helpless creatures, unable to do anything apart from faith in God. In His mercy, God has given humans the capacity to do many things, whether they believe in Him or not. But the Bible is clear that we are helpless to achieve righteousness. Look up the following verses, and summarize what they say about our righteousness and God's righteousness.

   A. Psalm 143:2
   B. Isaiah 64:6
   C. Jeremiah 23:6
   D. Romans 3:9, 10, 23
   E. 1 Corinthians 1:30, 31
   F. 2 Corinthians 5:21
   G. Philippians 3:8, 9

3. Divide the class into four groups. Each group should take one of God's four responses to Adam and Eve's sin identified in the lesson and discuss it. Then, through a skit, pantomime, or dramatic reading, each group should illustrate for the class the main point of the response.

4. The gospel is "the power of God for salvation to everyone who believes" (Romans 1:16, NASB). It is the story of the righteous Christ dying on the cross for undeserving sinners (1 Corinthians 1:17, 18). Using the *SDA Hymnal*, locate and write out key stanzas from three hymns that clearly point to the death of Jesus on the cross as the basis of our salvation.

5. Read what Jeremiah 25:15-17, Matthew 26:39-42, and Revelation 14:9, 10 say about a "cup." For each passage, in a brief paragraph, explain what the cup symbolizes. In a final paragraph, consider how Romans 5:9, 10 ties all three passages together.

- -

 Focus Questions

1. What are some of the ways we can sense God reaching out to us, even when we are not seeking Him?

2. In what ways do you think Satan is already a defeated foe because of the cross?

3. Apart from Calvary, do you know any other stories of someone giving up his/her life to save another person? What makes these stories so powerful?

4. Why did God choose the death of a lamb to symbolize Christ's sacrifice?

5. If God loves us the way this lesson says He does, why does He allow us to go through so many difficult times?

unit
3

God and the Human Family

Creation to Abraham

Unit three emphasizes God's unconditional and redeeming grace for the human family through experiences in the families of Adam, Noah, and Abraham. The introduction of sin, the Flood, and the Babel experience are covered. The lessons stress that through Jesus Christ, God's true character and love for the human family are revealed.

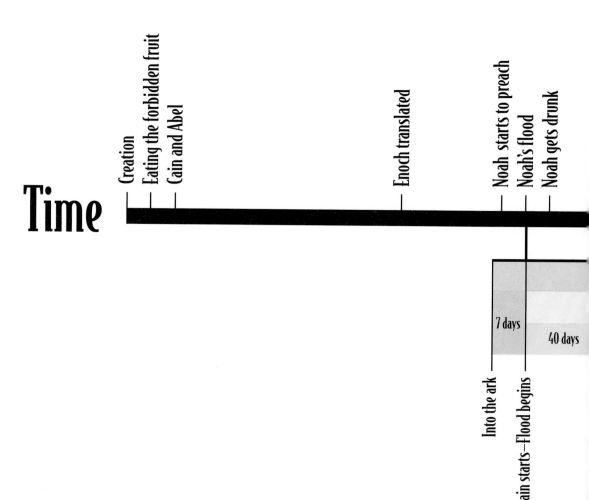

Time

Creation
Eating the forbidden fruit
Cain and Abel
Enoch translated
Noah starts to preach
Noah's flood
Noah gets drunk

7 days
40 days

Into the ark
Rain starts—Flood begins

line

Tower of Babel

Abraham leaves Ur

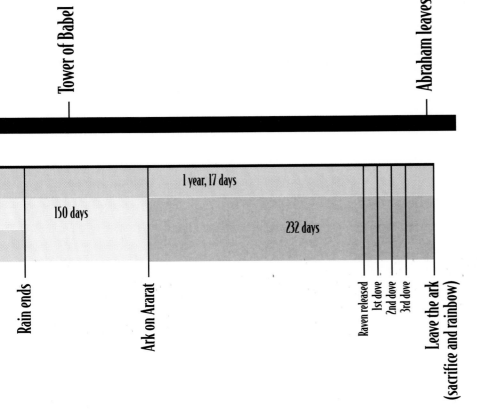

150 days

1 year, 17 days

232 days

Rain ends

Ark on Ararat

Raven released

1st dove

2nd dove

3rd dove

Leave the ark
(sacrifice and rainbow)

CHOICE

Anger can get you into trouble, but it's your pride that keeps you there
(Quips and Quotes).

STOP

Much More Than a Family Feud

Lesson Scripture: Genesis 4:1-17

"T hey're killing themselves!" the FBI agent in charge cried out to his co-workers watching in stunned disbelief as the headquarters of the religious community known as the Branch Davidians burst into flames and quickly burned to the ground. It is estimated that nearly eighty people, including seventeen children, lost their lives in the Waco, Texas, inferno of April 19, 1993. This agonizing standoff between agents of the Bureau of Alcohol, Tobacco, and Firearms and the residents of the Mount Carmel Compound lasted for fifty-one days. It included a deadly assortment of gun battles, numerous exchanges of questions and explanations, as well as a wide array of threats and demands from both sides.

Obviously, this deeply disturbing event aroused all kinds of human emotions. In the days and weeks that followed, grieving family members and friends, along with shocked Americans everywhere, wrestled with a variety of unanswered questions. What had gone wrong? Was the use of military force against a religious commune that seemed to be out of control the right or the wrong way to have handled this unusual situation?

What was the reason for the massive stockpiling of high-powered weapons, which caught the attention of government officials and set into motion an ill-fated raid on the settlement?

How could these deeply religious people so eagerly accept the bizarre teachings and immoral demands and practices of David Koresh, their self-proclaimed messiah? How could such ties of loyalty be developed that these people were apparently led to sacrifice their lives for their leader and the cause in which they believed?

Though these and many other questions still remain unanswered, the Waco catastrophe clearly demonstrates some important spiritual principles that ought to be thoughtfully considered.

First, we need to be aware that all people are involved in some kind of spiritual search. As creatures fashioned after God's image, there is within each of us a spiritual dimension, a hunger that seeks for ultimate answers, a desire to discover the meaning and purpose of our existence. There is also an inner longing to express one's spiritual convictions through outward forms of religion and worship.

A large number of new religious groups have come on the scene in our day. Many of them have been labeled as sects, or cults, because they promote certain beliefs and practices that are not biblical, but highly antagonistic toward other churches. The rapid rise and flourishing success of these new religious groups suggest that the spiritual needs of many people are not being satisfied by traditional denominations.

Another spiritual principle demonstrated by the Branch Davidians is that religion can be a very powerful force in a person's life—for good or for evil. Some people might resist the idea that a religion, of all things, can be depicted as evil and destructive. The Bible, however, makes it clear that a spiritual warfare is raging on our planet, involving two opposing powers, thus two rival religions. The controversy is between the forces of good and evil, between the true and the counterfeit. This means that religion and worship can either be an expression of one's relationship *with* God or of one's rebellion *against* Him. For this reason, the Bible admonishes us to first "test" the claims and beliefs of a religion before we embrace them, "to find out if the spirit they have comes from God" (1 John 4:1, TEV).

It is the *object* or *focus* of one's worship that determines the goodness and value of one's religion. In other words, what makes for a saving religion is determined by whether or not it is centered on Jesus Christ—our only Saviour from sin. Unfortunately, human pride and self-love can deceptively twist the worship of God into the worship of self, in which pleasing and relying upon self take priority over honoring and trusting God (see Romans 1:25). Each of us knows from personal experience the reality of this intense struggle within our hearts—the control center of our lives.

This spiritual controversy is vividly portrayed in the story of Cain and Abel. After sin had broken into this world, the Creator revealed to their parents, and thus to the two brothers, that there was only *one* provision for their salvation, only *one* Saviour provided for saving them. Despite this revelation from God, we find two altars in the first recorded worship service in the Bible. One had a lamb; the other was covered with fruit. These altars illustrate two opposing religions. In light of the deadly aftermath, it's obvious that this entire episode was much more than just a family feud. It was, in fact, the opening scene of what would become a global conflict between those who place their trust in God's offer of salvation and those who pin their hopes on their own efforts. Throughout human history, the *core* issue of religion has been whether acceptance with God can be found only through Christ's sacrifice or attained through human goodness, toil, and perseverance. The first family feud clearly demonstrates the answer.

This lesson is designed to guide you in your study of one of the most well-known narratives in the Bible—the Cain and Abel story. To be well-known, however, is not the same as being well understood. So be prepared to make many *new* discoveries and learn many *new* lessons from this very *old* but important Bible story.

Memory Focus

"By faith Abel offered God a better sacrifice than Cain did. By faith he was commended as a righteous man, when God spoke well of his offerings. And by faith he still speaks, even though he is dead" (Hebrews 11:4, NIV).

. . . .

 # Into the Bible

1. During Adam and Eve's lifetime, they had many "sons and daughters" (Genesis 5:4), but only events in the lives of Cain and Abel are recorded in the Bible. The fact that the presentation of their offerings to God is the only biblical story concerning these two brothers should indicate to us its extreme importance and relevance.

   Read Genesis 4:1-16, and answer the following questions:
   A. Describe the offering that each brother presented to the Lord.
   B. What did Abel's offering cause him to realize, which Cain would not need to confront through his offering? (See Leviticus 17:11; Isaiah 53:6; 1 Peter 1:18, 19.)
   C. Describe God's response to each offering.
   D. What indication had God already given concerning the kind of offering acceptable to Him? (See Genesis 3:21.)
   E. What does 1 John 3:12 say regarding Cain and his offering?
   F. What is said about Abel and his offering in Hebrews 11:4?

2. Genesis 4 records the first conflict among family members. Cain's rebellion and separation from God brought about the rift between him and his brother. And it established an important spiritual principle: The kind of relationship we have with God will determine the quality of our relationships with others.

Read the following texts, and write the insights they give regarding the principle stated in the preceding paragraph.

    A. 1 John 4:20, 21
    B. Proverbs 16:7
    C. 2 Corinthians 5:17-20

3. The Cain and Abel narrative illustrates a spiritual theme that permeates all Scripture. This issue centers around the ongoing conflict between truth and error, between Christ-centered religion and human-centered religion, between authentic spirituality and the counterfeit.

    All religions, whether good or evil, focus on certain basic beliefs and practices. The most common characteristics include the worship of a god, special powers and miracles, prophets and leaders, laws and commandments, and their beliefs and primary message.

    In this activity you will study biblical texts that relate to these and other spiritual features that characterize both true and false religions. Write out a summary statement for each text, or in some cases, group of texts.

    A. 2 Thessalonians 2:4
        1 Chronicles 16:25, 26
    B. Matthew 24:5
        Matthew 24:24
    C. Matthew 7:15
        Matthew 24:11
    D. Ephesians 6:12
    E. 1 John 4:1-3
    F. Matthew 7:21-23
    G. Revelation 13:14
        Revelation 16:14
    H. Galatians 1:6-8
        2 Corinthians 11:13-15

4. Several explanations have been offered for why God rejected Cain's offering. The three most common ones are:

    • Cain's offering was inferior and of poor quality.

- Cain's offering did not symbolize Christ's sacrifice.
- Cain had a rebellious and defiant attitude toward God.

Using the texts below, identify personal lessons that can be applied to your worship and relationship with God.

A. Genesis 4:7
B. Genesis 22:7, 8
C. Leviticus 17:11; Hebrews 9:22
D. John 14:6
E. Romans 3:23-25
F. Hebrews 11:4

 **Projects**

1. WRITE A LETTER: Compose a letter that Cain might have written to his parents and his younger brothers and sisters back home, explaining his side of the story regarding his offering and God's rejection and/or the slaying of Abel.
2. ESTABLISH A DEFENSE: A friend of yours tells you that if you're sincere in what you believe and you live the best life that you can, then it doesn't matter what religion you belong to. If you do this, you will be saved, no matter what your religion might be. What is your answer? Write a paper defining what you believe and defending it from Scripture.
3. CONDUCT A SURVEY: Take a survey by interviewing at least five people in your neighborhood and in your church or school. (You may wish to work in pairs.) Ask them the following three questions:
   A. Have you ever read or heard about the story of Cain and Abel?
   B. Do you believe it is a true story or a fable?
   C. What do you think is the main lesson of this story?
   Write a report of the results of your survey, and share your reactions and conclusions with the class.
4. EXPRESS A VIEWPOINT: Write a thought paper on one of the following questions:

A. Why does God allow good people to suffer?
B. Why does life seem so unfair?
C. Where is God when things go wrong in my life?
D. How can a good God allow bad things to happen?
E. What value or purpose is there in pain and suffering?
F. Should I praise the Lord no matter what happens to me?

 # Focus Questions

1. What did God mean when He said to Cain, "Your brother's blood cries out to me from the ground"? (You may compare this to the statement in Hebrews 11:4, "By faith he [Abel] still speaks, even though he is dead.")
2. Why do you suppose God asked Cain where his brother was?
3. What was Cain trying to say when he asked God, "Am I my brother's keeper"?
4. What does it mean to be our brother's keeper? Who is my brother?
5. Do you think that the curses God pronounced on Cain and the ground are something God is directly responsible for, or did they come about primarily as the natural consequences of Cain's wrongdoing and his separation from God?
6. Do you see anything significant about the fact that the world's first murderer was also the first builder of a city?
7. In Genesis 4:14 Cain accuses God of driving him away from God's presence. Verse 16, however, says that Cain, on his own, went out from God's presence. Which one describes what actually happened? How does one leave the presence of God?
8. Why does it seem necessary for God to have protected Cain with some kind of "mark"? Who, most likely, would God have been protecting him from?
9. Why did God choose not to intervene on Abel's behalf and spare his life?
10. What are some good, practical suggestions for resolving family conflicts?

ROOTS

If you want the future to be different from the present, study the past
(The Daily Walk).

Adam's Family Tree

Lesson Scripture: Genesis 4:15–5:32

THE STORY OF OUR LIFE

It was my turn to pick a present from under the Christmas tree. I chose a large package with my name on it. I opened the card and read "Merry Christmas from Mom." I tore off the wrapping paper and opened the gold foil box. Under many layers of fine tissue paper was a large photo album.

I turned back the cover and read the passage in my mother's handwriting:

I have tried to live a bit of yesterday in both writing and pictures. First your father's and my ancestors, then our parents, then our lives as we were growing up, and finally the lives of you children as you joined the march of time.

The inscription continued, *Another purpose for this album is to fulfill the following saying in your life: "There are two things you can give your children: one is roots, the other is wings."*

My family and I spent a good deal of that Christmas morning exploring our heritage and shared memories through this photographic family tree.

The making and researching of family trees is called genealogy, and it is one of humankind's oldest pursuits. For my family, it was a way to meet our ancestors and relive significant family events. Ancient pagan peoples made genealogies to trace their origins to animals or plants. Luke traces Jesus' ancestry back to Adam, and Julius Caesar traced his own back to the goddess Venus.

Some people have used genealogies to prove they descended from famous historical characters. The emperor of Ethiopia once made a family tree to prove he was a descendant of King Solomon and the queen of Sheba.

Genealogies have been used in England to verify royal blood, legal rights to property, and the collection of taxes. Alex Haley wrote his bestselling novel *Roots,* a genealogy of sorts, to give his people a sense of pride and belonging. Mormons compose genealogies because they believe they should be baptized for all those who died as non-Mormons.

No doubt there have been times when you've wondered about the real meaning and purpose of "Adam's family tree." The genealogies recorded by Moses in Genesis 4 and 5 reveal important concepts that may not be learned in any other way. At the same time, they can also be easily misunderstood. Problems may arise when Genesis is viewed as a tool to deal with scientific matters.

An example of such misuse is when genealogies are used to determine the age of the earth by adding up the ages of all those named on the list. When biblical genealogies are examined and compared, they are often shown to be incomplete. Genesis 4 and 5 may only contain a sample of those who actually lived from Adam to Noah. This indicates that the writer was primarily concerned with spiritual issues rather than time lines and chronology.

Moses wrote the genealogies in Genesis to give roots and wings to a slave people coming out of Egypt. The roots were their origin as God's creatures and their ancestors' pilgrimage with God. The wings offered hope and comfort to those who walk with God, like Enoch and Abraham. In the end, all the biblical genealogies finally point to the One who gives wings of hope to the whole human race, for whom "a Son is born."

 **Memory Focus**

"By faith Enoch was taken from this life, so that he did not experience death; he could not be found, because God had taken him away. For before he was taken, he was commended as one who pleased God. And without faith it is impossible to please God, because anyone who comes to him must believe that he exists and that he rewards those who earnestly seek him" (Hebrews 11:5, 6, NIV).

. . . .

 Into the Bible

1. Read the text, and respond to the following questions:

   A. Read Exodus 20:4-6. What does this text say about the long-range effect of parents' attitudes and actions on children and later generations?

   B. Read the two genealogies in Genesis 4:16-24; 4:25–5:32. How do the details given about different people illustrate the effect parents can have on their children?

2. There are many traditional ideas about why Enoch was translated. What does the Bible say? Study Hebrews 11:5, 6 and 39, 40; then answer the following questions:

   A. According to these four verses, what is the basis of Enoch's salvation? Of others' salvation in Hebrews 11?

   B. Paul writes: "Only together with us would they be made perfect" (Hebrews 11:40, NIV). Compare Hebrews 10:14 and 12:1-3. What does *perfection* mean in these verses?

3. What does the Bible say about Enoch's relationship with God and some of the conditions that existed in his day?

   A. *Enoch's relationship with God:* How do the following verses describe Enoch's relationship with God?

(1) Genesis 5:24; Amos 3:3

(2) Hebrews 11:5, 6

B. *Enoch's world:* According to the genealogies in Genesis 4 and 5 (4:17-22; 5:3-24), Enoch was the seventh generation from Adam on the side of Seth, and Lamech was the seventh generation from Adam on the side of Cain. This suggests that Enoch and Lamech lived at about the same time.

(1) Read Genesis 4:19-24. Describe Lamech's moral character. How did he handle conflicts with other people?

(2) a. Read Jude 14–16. What was the typical moral character of the wicked of Enoch's day?

b. Read Hebrews 11:5. Contrast Enoch's character with the wicked of his day. What bearing did this have on God translating Enoch?

 Projects

1. To "walk with God!" Genesis 5:22 says: "Enoch walked with God." This implies going beyond "just being religious." Read *Patriarchs and Prophets*, pages 84-87. Then write a personal definition of what it would mean in your life to walk with God. Colossians 3:12-17 may be helpful in getting you started.

2. Chart the ages of the first twenty patriarchs named in the Bible. Your teacher will provide you with the chart and instructions.

 Focus Questions

1. Why does the Bible describe Seth as being born in Adam's "own likeness, after his image" when Adam was created "in the image of God"?

2. What do you think it means when the Bible says that Enoch walked with God after he begat Methuselah?

3. Why do some people believe that Enoch reached sinless perfection before he was translated? How does this idea affect your view of salvation? Of final events?

4. What do you think is the basic purpose of Lamech's song in Genesis 4:23, 24?

5. Why does Moses give such details regarding Lamech's family, while nothing is said of the other descendants of Cain?

6. Why do you think God offered to protect Cain after slaying Abel, but not Lamech after he murdered a man?

CARPE DIEM
(SEIZE THE DAY)
Between tomorrow's dream and yesterday's regret is today's opportunity
(Quips and Quotes).

lesson 18

The Flood and Noah's Family

Lesson Scripture: Genesis 6-9

SAME EVIDENCE, TWO VIEWS

The Bible is straightforward about a flood. However, there are opposing viewpoints about this worldwide catastrophe. The evolutionist theorists state that there were various localized floods that were the result of natural causes. They say these could be the result of a meteorite striking the earth or the changing of the ocean level due to climate or the rising or sinking of the earth's surface or the cycles of erosion caused by water, wind, or ice. The creationist viewpoint promotes the biblical account of the Flood caused by God's decision and control.

Though their conclusions conflict, the proponents of each viewpoint use the same evidence from geology, the study of the earth's formation, to support their position. The following is a list of evidence used:

1. The layers of rocks called sedimentary rocks or strata, which were laid down by the movement of water.
2. The marine deposits in the mountains located great distances from present oceans.
3. The worldwide spread of deposits of similar earth materials.
4. The worldwide extinctions of large vertebrate land and marine life in a short time period.
5. Sedimentary deposits, called "turbidity currents," that moved down the slopes very rapidly at the end of the continental shelf.

171

6. The lack of erosion between sediment layers, indicating that it happened in a short period of time.

So who is interpreting the evidence correctly—the evolutionists or creationists?

The evolutionists rely on scientific observation alone to explain the evidence of the flood or floods. The creationists, on the other hand, attempt to harmonize what is discovered in nature with the revealed account of the Flood found in Genesis. But whose method is correct—the evolutionists' or creationists'?

Each person's interpretation of the evidence and the method used are based on one's worldview. What is the main cause of the Flood, nature or God? Is the Flood a part of a cause-and-effect system of nature or part of God's plan? Is the source for the answers found in science or revelation?

The answers to these questions cannot be scientifically determined. The only answer is faith. What one chooses to believe is based upon the reasonableness of the evidence. But which viewpoint is to be accepted by faith—the evolutionists' or the creationists'?

The major difference between the evolutionists and the creationists is their theories of the origin of this world. The evolutionists believe the physical elements of this world have always been in existence. Furthermore, they believe that by some evolutionary process, the world and its inhabitants have developed to their present condition. The creationists believe all the reasonable evidence points to an eternal God, who by personal involvement created this world and its inhabitants.

As creationists, therefore, we believe the evidence for the Flood can be discovered in nature and understood from God's revealed Word—the Bible. We try to harmonize the evidence found in nature with the story account found in Genesis. But science and Scripture have different perspectives. Science focuses primarily on objective data, such as what, when, where, and how, while Scripture's main focus adds the dimension of why it happened.

Regardless of the scientific evidence for the Flood, the Genesis account of the Flood is more than science. It is a story about people who make choices and experiment with a way of living. It is an account of God, His concerns, and His will for those people.

A REVIEW OF GENESIS

A review of Genesis, chapters 1 to 5, is needed to understand the context of the Flood. Genesis is about God, the Creator of this world. When He had finished Creation, He saw that "it was very good." The crowning act was the creation of man and woman. The Lord gave man and woman life, the Sabbath, marriage, the Garden of Eden, and a personal relationship with Himself.

Behind the story of Genesis is the great conflict between God and Satan. This conflict crashes into God's new creation with the first couple's fateful choice. They accept Satan's reasoning; sin and its consequences become a part of creation. The man and woman now experience personal shame, fear, mistrust, banishment, and ultimately death. But into this dark picture of despair, God gives the promise of redemption—"I will put enmity between you [the serpent] and the woman" (Genesis 3:15, NIV). There will be conflict, but in the end, victory. This promise hits home with awful reality in the next chapter, Genesis 4. Cain kills Abel because God accepted Abel's sacrifice, which revealed his faith in the promise of a divine Sacrifice for sin. He leaves God's presence and becomes a restless wanderer. But another son, Seth, is born to take the place of Abel. Cain and Seth become the fathers of two genealogies. The descendants of Cain continue to reflect his rebellion against God, whereas Seth's descendants remain loyal to God.

REASON FOR THE FLOOD

Genesis chapter 6 explains why God decided to destroy the earth by water. Seth's descendants should have maintained their separation from Cain's, but they did not. There was intermingling and marriage between good and evil. "The sons of God saw that the daughters of men were beautiful, and they married any of them they chose" (verse 2, NIV).

What difference did this make? God gave humankind the freedom of choice—"to think and to do." Therefore, these people had the freedom to marry whomever they chose. True. But the misuse of that freedom had serious consequences.

These unholy alliances threatened the very existence of creation. The evil they spawned was the reason for the Flood. Through these marriages, the worship of God was forsaken until "every inclination of the thoughts of [their hearts] was only evil all the time" (verse 5, NIV). This persistent evil led to great wickedness, corruption, and violence. God's heart was filled with pain, and He grieved that He had made humans. He had created something very good. Now it was very wicked. So God decided to "wipe mankind . . . from the face of the earth" (verse 7, NIV).

"But Noah found favor in the eyes of the Lord." There was one person who, by faith in God's promise, was "righteous [and] . . . blameless among the people of his time, and he walked with God" (verses 8, 9, NIV). And so God acted in Noah's behalf. He made a way of escape for anyone who, in faith, would enter the safety of the ark. Only eight in Noah's family made that choice. Through Noah's faith, God carried out His merciful plan to save the future of humanity. Through the ark and the Flood, God was able to preserve the line of Adam and the light of the gospel. ⚡

 Memory Focus

"By faith Noah, when warned about things not yet seen, in holy fear built an ark to save his family. By his faith he condemned the world and became heir of the righteousness that comes by faith" (Hebrews 11:7, NIV).

. . . .

 Into the Bible

1. In Genesis, the character of Noah is vividly contrasted with the antediluvians (people who lived before the Flood). On the worksheet provided by your teacher, do the following:

   A. Make two lists, one describing Noah's actions and attitudes, the other dealing with the actions and attitudes of the antediluvians.
   B. Review the characteristics of Noah you listed in 1A, and write a summary paragraph describing the kind of man you think he was.

2. In discussing the last days, Jesus said, "As it was in the days of Noah, so it will be at the coming of the Son of Man" (Matthew 24:37, NIV). Use the worksheet your teacher will provide to show this comparison.

3. Although Noah and the antediluvians play important roles in the Flood story, the leading character in this life-and-death drama is God Himself.

   A. Read Genesis 6; 8:1, 20-22; 9, and list the attitude and actions of God.
   B. How do these divine attitudes and activities help us understand the plan of salvation (the outworking of His justice and mercy) that God provides for all people?

4. Read the following texts, and provide the information called for.

A. Genesis 7:10, 11—The source of the water.
B. Genesis 7:11 and 8:13-15—The length of time that Noah and his family were in the ark.

 **Projects**

1. Being as creative and imaginative as possible, sketch a picture of A, B, C, or D below to show how you think the ark looked:

   A. During its construction.
   B. On the waters at the height of the storm.
   C. On Mount Ararat following the Flood.
   D. How it may look at the present time.

2. Imagine yourself as a reporter for the *Mount Ararat Daily News*. You have been assigned to write a feature article concerning the public's response to Noah's building the ark and his straightforward warning about the end of the world. At the time you are writing, the ark had been completed, and there is a rumor that Noah is about to make an important announcement concerning coming events. As you attend this meeting, what do you hear and see? What is the mood and attitude of the people? How do they react to Noah's warning of doom and his assertion that the ark is the only way of salvation from the waters? Using Genesis 6:1-13 and the following statements from *Patriarchs and Prophets*, pages 90-104, write your feature article describing the antediluvians. Incorporate the following points:

   The antediluvians (people who lived before the Flood):

   A. "Endeavored to excel one another in beautifying their dwellings" (p. 90).
   B. "Came to deny His [God's] existence" (p. 91).
   C. "Delighted in destroying the life of animals" (p. 92).
   D. "Came to regard human life with astonishing indifference" (p. 92).
   E. Were unwilling to renounce their sins . . . [and] turn to God with true repentance" (p. 95).

F. "Declared that the divine law was no longer in force" (p. 96).
G. Declared "it was contrary to the character of God to punish transgression" (p. 96).
H. Regarded Noah as "a wild fanatic" (p. 96).
I. "Manifested their contempt for the warning of God by doing just as they had done before the warning [of Noah] was given" (p. 97).
J. Took God's "gifts without gratitude to the Giver" (p. 101).
K. Debased "themselves by indulging appetite without restraint" (p. 101).
L. "Gave themselves up to exciting amusements and festivities" (p. 103).
M. "Declared that it was impossible for the world to be destroyed by water" (p. 103).
N. "Found out too late that their wisdom was foolishness" (p. 104).

3. Write an article titled "The Return of the Antediluvian." The objective of the article is to compare today's moral conditions with the pre-Flood world. Use specific examples from current news events (see also 2 Timothy 3:1-5).

Focus Questions

1. In what way is the ark an appropriate symbol of Christ in God's plan of salvation?
2. How could a God of love destroy the world by a flood?
3. Was the ark a large boat or simply a huge box that could float?
4. Why did God forbid the eating of flesh with blood after the Flood?
5. Do you think Noah's curse on Canaan was a punishment for sin or a description of the consequences of sin?
6. Why do you think Ham's actions were treated so severely? What might this event have to say regarding the effects of evil within a family (see Exodus 20:5)?

AMBITION
Every generation has its own Tower of Babel (Gordon Kainer).

Babel and the World's Family

Lesson Scripture: Genesis 11:1-9

The following experience is recorded in the diary of my year as a student missionary. It is dated January 14, 1979.

DON'T FOLLOW ME . . . I'M LOST

"Oh pain! Lloyd woke us up at 5:15 in the morning. 'We must find the legendary Amoro Mountain,' he said. We ate, broke camp, and loaded up. It started to rain hard and rained till five o'clock in the evening. We were soaked in seconds.

"We hiked in the direction of the Petasamo River. On the way, at least 20 to 30 yellow monkeys were sighted flying and jumping through the air from limb to limb. Blue butterflies were everywhere. We finally came to the river and crossed it. But here we made our mistake.

"Edgar advised us to take a different path, which led us to another river. We crossed it four times, then discovered we were going the wrong way. So we started bushwhacking. I mean bushwhacking! We were deep in the Bolivian jungle with its vines and dense undergrowth. We chopped and walked through this jungle for three hours.

"Finally, we found a hunting cabin to rest in. Lloyd and I oriented ourselves by map and compass and within a half-hour were out in the rain again walking. After two hours, we came to the Petasamo River again. Putting our packs over our heads, we crossed over it again. From then on we moved upriver, often by swinging from vine to vine or wading chest deep in the water."

Why did we ever follow Edgar's advice? God has endowed us with a "power akin to that of the Creator—individuality, power to think and to do."[1] Why didn't we use this power? It would have saved five tiring hours of bushwhacking through the Bolivian jungle! If only we had consulted our map first. Maps are a vital part of life. They help us understand our surroundings and reach our destination. Without a map, we are at the mercy of others for directions or left to our own wanderings.

DECISION DETERMINES DESTINY

We have many types of maps: road maps, topographical maps, city maps, flier charts, and political maps. These are physical maps. Genesis presents another type of map, a genealogy. This map presents two lines of people found in history.

Notice on the following chart how each group has the same starting point. Yet what a different destiny. The lineage of Cain decided to forge their own path. They followed the map of

self-sufficiency, unbelief, and rebellion. This way ended in destruction by water and fire. The lineage of Seth chose the path blazed by God. They followed the map of submission, faith, and obedience. This way ends in salvation.

No one can avoid this genealogical map. But each person has the ability to decide which path he or she will follow. Moses told the Israelites as they prepared to enter the Promised Land, "See, I set before you today life and prosperity, death and destruction. For I command you today to love the Lord your God, to walk in his ways, and to keep his commands, decrees and laws; then you will live and increase, and the Lord your God will bless you in the land you are entering to possess. But if your heart turns away and you are not obedient, and if you are drawn away to bow down to other gods and worship them, I declare to you this day that you will certainly be destroyed" (Deuteronomy 30:15-18, NIV).

GOD'S LOVE

God is Creator and Redeemer of all. He works with all human genealogies. John 3:16,

---

[1] White, Ellen, *Education.* Boise, Idaho: Pacific Press, 1952, 17.

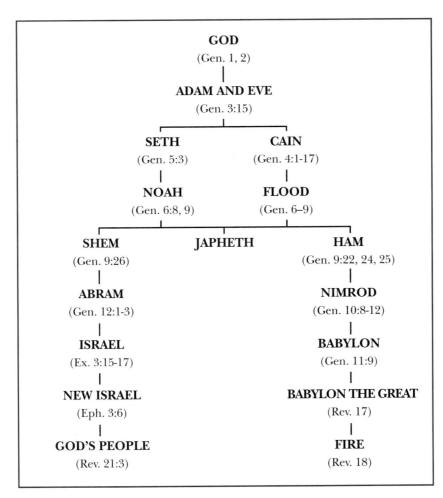

GOD
(Gen. 1, 2)

ADAM AND EVE
(Gen. 3:15)

SETH
(Gen. 5:3)

CAIN
(Gen. 4:1-17)

NOAH
(Gen. 6:8, 9)

FLOOD
(Gen. 6–9)

SHEM
(Gen. 9:26)

JAPHETH

HAM
(Gen. 9:22, 24, 25)

ABRAM
(Gen. 12:1-3)

NIMROD
(Gen. 10:8-12)

ISRAEL
(Ex. 3:15-17)

BABYLON
(Gen. 11:9)

NEW ISRAEL
(Eph. 3:6)

BABYLON THE GREAT
(Rev. 17)

GOD'S PEOPLE
(Rev. 21:3)

FIRE
(Rev. 18)

17 says, "For God so loved the world that he gave his one and only Son, that whoever believes in him shall not perish but have eternal life. For God did not send his Son into the world to condemn the world, but to save the world through him" (NIV). His unrelenting love and re-deeming grace still reach out to those who have chosen Cain's legacy. His love even took Him to a cross to save all of humanity.

LIFE MAP

We have learned about genealogical maps. Another invisible map is called a "Life

Map"[2]—a set of internal values or principles that govern our behavior. This map guides us from within. It influences our every action, belief, attitude, motive, and even emotion. Each person has one of these maps. However, one is not born with this map but is responsible for developing it. It takes a lifetime of effort, dedication, revising,[3] and trust in God to develop an accurate Life Map.

Since the fall of Adam and Eve, many Life Maps have been developed and tried. A Humanist Map says: "Trust yourself." A Materialist Map says: "Please yourself." But a Christian Map says: "Follow Jesus." The struggle to determine which one is accurate and correct is often painful. Proverbs 14:12 suggests the right map is important when it says, "There is a way that seems right to a man, but in the end it leads to death."

Your Life Map has been shaped by parents, church, school, and society to this point. But you have a "power to think and to do"—now you must shape your own map. To use this power, you must "be thinkers and not mere reflectors of other men's thought."[4] Solomon noted, "As he thinketh in his heart, so is he" (Proverbs 23:7). Remember, life is a jungle out there. You need to have and use an accurate map to reach your destination.

In the story of Genesis 11:1-9, a particular Life Map is tried. Because it is a common Life Map, it needs to be studied and evaluated before it is accepted or rejected. Studying this passage provides an opportunity to develop an accurate map to help you reach the best destination—heaven.

[2] David Bender, *Constructing a Life Philosophy* (St. Paul, Minn.: Greenhaven Press, Inc., 1985), 18.

[3] Bender, 19.

[4] *Education*, 17.

Memory Focus

"There is a way that seems right to a man, but in the end it leads to death" (Proverbs 14:12, NIV).

 Into the Bible

1. A. Read Genesis 11:1-9. Then compile the following information:
        (1) Who are the main characters in the story?
        (2) When did the story occur?
        (3) Where did the events take place?
        (4) What actions by the main characters took place in the story?
        (5) Why did the main characters act as they did? (What were their motives?)
    B. Imagine you're a reporter for the *Babel Times*. What do you see, hear, etc.? Rewrite the story as a two- to three-paragraph news article, using the information you gathered in 1A.
2. Read Genesis 8:21; 9:1, 9-16; 11:1-9. Notice the promises and instructions God made to humanity and, further, how the people of Babel defied God. Now, imagine God has called you to be His messenger to Babel. Based on the texts above, write a two- to three-paragraph letter you would send to persuade the people of Babel to return to God.
3. The Tower of Babel was built on the plain of Shinar in the region of Babylon. The word *Babel* sounds like the Hebrew word for "confusion." The Bible uses this Babel experience (Genesis 11) as the starting point for "Babylon." In Scripture Babylon becomes a symbol for a human-centered, self-dependent system in defiance of God.
    A. Read Genesis 11:1-9. Write out the verse that shows that even at its beginning Babel (Babylon) was a system of salvation by works in which people rejected God's offer of salvation and tried to save themselves.
    B. Read Daniel 3:1-6. How does Babylon treat those who do not choose to worship as it dictates?
    C. According to Revelation 18:2, 3, how widespread is Babylon's influence of spiritual confusion?
    D. Read Revelation 14:8. What finally happens to "Babylon," this system of dependence on self rather than trust in God?
4. Read Genesis 11:5-9 to answer the following questions:

A. What did God do before He scattered the people of Shinar?
B. What caused the dispersal of the people of Shinar?
C. What was the result of this separation?

 Projects

1. **LIFE MAP:** Read the Life Map section in the narrative again to understand the concept of a Life Map. A Life Map is a set of internal principles or values that govern our behavior. This map guides us over the terrain of life. The map's accuracy determines whether we reach our destination or not. Since we are not born with a Life Map, we spend our lifetime developing our own.

   It is helpful to know that others have developed life maps and have left a record of their discoveries for our benefit. King Solomon had the opportunity during his lifetime to follow several different maps. Because of this, we are going to let him show us various Life Maps.

   A. Solomon records his analysis of these Life Maps in his book Ecclesiastes. Study the following Life Maps, and write out Solomon's evaluation of each one:
   (1) Wisdom and knowledge (Ecclesiastes 1:12-18)
   (2) Pleasure (Ecclesiastes 2:1-11)
   (3) Work, toil (Ecclesiastes 2:17-21)
   (4) Popularity (Ecclesiastes 4:13-16)
   (5) Riches (Ecclesiastes 5:13-16)
   B. Read Ecclesiastes 12:13, 14, and describe the Life Map that has meaning.
   C. Solomon indicates that all Life Maps are meaningless unless they lead to God. Analyze why a Life Map that includes God provides meaning to life.

2. **MAJOR TOWERS TODAY:** Read *Patriarchs and Prophets,* pages 123, 124. Carefully analyze the meaning of the phrase "There are tower builders in our time." Clearly, the Tower of Babel can be a metaphor for any human-centered system or lifestyle.

Every generation or society has its own "towers of Babel." Write a short report on a major "tower" in the world today that separates people from God. (Any major worldview, philosophy, religious system, or lifestyle is a possible major tower.)

3. **SEPARATION:**
   A. Write down what comes to your mind when you think of the word *separation.*
   B. Is separation good or bad? Explain.
   C. Since God caused separation at the Tower of Babel, separation must be good. Agree or disagree? Explain.
   D. If God separates people, should we try to unite them?
   E. If we are to unite people, upon what basis can we do so?
   F. How can this act of separating people be part of God's plan of salvation, especially when it is His plan to unite all things in Christ?

 Focus Questions

1. Do you think independence, self-sufficiency, and pride are wrong and harmful? Explain.
2. Why did God disperse (scatter) the people at the Tower of Babel?
3. Does God always investigate the activities of humankind before He judges them? Explain.
4. Based on this story, do we really have freedom of choice?
5. What modern technologies might become "towers" that impair our relationship with God? How might they do so?
6. How would the Babel philosophy of self-sufficiency and independence affect the social issues of equality and homelessness?
7. If I accept the Babel philosophy, how would I act in the following situations: on a date, at work, in church, playing sports?
8. In what ways was "confusing the language" beneficial to the people? How did God's judgment help save them?
9. How does God act in judgment against the "Tower of Babel" in our day?

PERSISTENCE

Many of life's failures are people who did not realize how close they were
to success when they gave up *(Quips and Quotes).*

lesson 20

Abraham: His Move and Mission

Lesson Scripture: Genesis 12:1-7

UR TURN

The young maiden falls into the arms of the strong, handsome hero who has just rescued her. Can't you just picture this romantic scene in your mind's theater? Haven't you daydreamed of living such an event? The romance, action, adventure, and danger all twisted together?

As a kid, I loved to read the *We Were There . . .* series. *We Were There at Pearl Harbor* and *We Were There With Byrd at the South Pole* were my favorites. I experienced the adventure of yesterday's heroes. I became an actor. I became a hero.

William Shakespeare, a man of soaring imagination, said, "All the world's a stage, and all the men and women merely players. They have their exits and their entrances. And one man in his time plays many parts."[1] Yesterday's heroes have exited. Now it's our turn to be actors on this world's stage. We can be today's heroes. But what will be our parts? How will we respond to our roles? How well will we perform? How will we be accepted by the audience and critics?

Like any actor, we want our moments on this world's stage to go well. We pray for no mistakes or blunders. We want life's audience to admire, applaud, and respect us. At the end of our performances, we want to bow and say like Paul, "I have fought the good fight, I have finished

---

[1] *As You Like It*, act 2, scene 7.

187

the race, I have kept the faith. Now there is in store for me the crown of righteousness" (2 Timothy 4:7, 8, NIV).

Some of us want to camp on the stage. We are thrilled by its sounds and sights. Others are merely passing through, like the heroes of Hebrews 11: "They admitted that they were aliens and strangers on earth. People who say such things show that they are looking for a country of their own. If they had been thinking of the country they had left, they would have had opportunity to return. Instead, they were longing for a better country—a heavenly one. Therefore God is not ashamed to be called their God, for he has prepared a city for them" (verses 13-16, NIV).

We are fortunate to have the history and examples of past actors on life's stage to examine. We can evaluate their achievements and failures. We can avoid their mistakes and copy their successes and victories.

ABRAM'S BACKGROUND

Abram is one of the greatest actors and heroes of the past.

His stage life was one of adventure, danger, romance, conflict, mistakes, and victories. Today, he is admired, applauded, and respected as the father of the Muslims, the Jews, and the Christians.

He was named Abram at birth, meaning "high father." He was a descendant of Shem, a son of Noah. He grew up in Ur in the land of the Chaldeans (Iraq). He married his half-sister, Sarai. He moved with his father, Terah, to Haran (Syria).

Abram was seventy-five when the Lord told him, "Leave your country, your people and your father's household and go to the land I will show you. . . . To your offspring I will give this land" (Genesis 12:1, 7). God chose Abram because he was responsive, dissatisfied with his heathen environment, and ready to worship the one true God, Yahweh. God had a role for Abram. "I will make you into a great nation . . . and you will be a blessing" (Genesis 12:2, NIV). The following map gives the likely route Abram took to his new home.

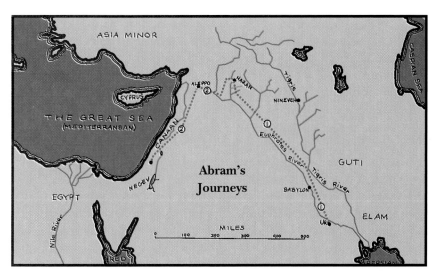

THE LAND OF CANAAN

The land to which God sent Abram was Canaan. The map below indicates the borders of Canaan, according to Genesis 10:19 and 15:17-21.

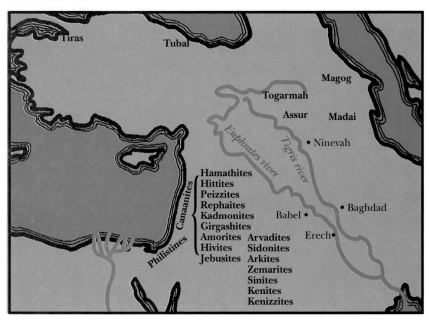

Scripture says Canaan was "the most beautiful of all lands" (Ezekiel 20:6, NIV). The land was good, a spacious land flowing with milk and honey. There were many streams, pools of water, and springs flowing in the valleys and hills. It produced wheat, barley, vines, figs, pomegranates, and olives. It was said that its rock was iron, and copper could be found in the hills. It was a land that lacked nothing. But above all, "it is a land the Lord your God cares for; the eyes of the Lord your God are continually on it from the beginning of the year to its end" (Deuteronomy 11:12, NIV).

The land of Canaan was beautiful, but its inhabitants were wicked. It was the land of the Kenites, Kenizzites, Kadmonites, Hittites, Perizzites, Rephaites, Amorites, Canaanites, Girgashites, and Jebusites. They were pagans who built altars, sacred stones, Asherah poles, and idols. They prostituted themselves to their gods. They even burned their sons and daughters in sacrificial fires to their gods. They practiced divination, sorcery, and interpreting omens. They engaged in witchcraft, casting spells, and consulting the dead. They were perversely immoral.

THE PROMISE

Abram was told to go into this land of physical beauty and spiritual ugliness. However, it was God's land, and He had a plan for it. Abram was to be His witness and agent of restoration. Before Abram left on his journey, God gave this promise: "I will make you into a great nation and I will bless you; I will make your name great, and you will be a blessing. I will bless those who bless you, and whoever curses you I will curse; and all peoples on earth will be blessed through you" (Genesis 12:2, 3, NIV).

ABRAM AS A MODEL

Abram was a model for his

descendants, the greatest of whom is Jesus Christ. Like Abram, Jesus left His country, people, and father and journeyed to a wicked world to bring restoration. His name and nation are great. Most importantly, Jesus provided the greatest blessing this world has ever known: the forgiveness of sins through the sacrifice of Himself.

Abram was an example for us. It is our turn to be actors on this life's stage. We are also called to be God's witnesses and agents of restoration. Will we follow in Abram's footsteps? The Into the Bible questions are designed to help you understand God's promise to Abram. ⅄

. . . .

Memory Focus

"The Lord had said to Abram, 'Leave your country, your people and your father's household and go to the land I will show you. I will make you into a great nation and I will bless you; I will make your name great, and you will be a blessing. I will bless those who bless you, and whoever curses you I will curse; and all peoples on earth will be blessed through you'" (Genesis 12:1-3, NIV).

 **Into the Bible**

1. God made Abram a promise in Genesis 12:2, 3, 7. List the six elements of the promise.
2. God promised Abram, Isaac, and Jacob, "You will be a blessing . . . and all nations on earth will be blessed through your offspring." God did not immediately indicate how this would be accomplished. This question studies the two key words of the promise: *blessing* and *offspring.* As you study these two words, you will discover how God intended to fulfill this promise.

    A. Examine the following texts to identify who Abram's offspring might be:
       (1) Genesis 21:12   (4) Matthew 1:1
       (2) Genesis 28:10-14   (5) Galatians 3:28, 29
       (3) Deuteronomy 10:12, 15

    B. How were Abram's offspring to be a blessing to all people and nations? Examine the following texts, and list the possibilities:
       (1) 1 Chronicles 16:8, 9, 23   (4) Isaiah 58:6, 7
       (2) Psalm 72:4, 12-14   (5) Matthew 5:14-16
       (3) Isaiah 43:10

· ·

 **Project**

Imagine you are Abram. God appears to you this evening and says, "Leave your country, your people, and your parents' household, and go to the land I will show you. I will make you into a great nation, and I will bless you, I will make your name great, and you will be a blessing. I will bless those who bless you, and whoever curses you I will curse; and all peoples on earth will be blessed through you. I will give this land to your offspring."

In not more than one page, record your reaction. The following questions may be helpful to stimulate your thoughts, but they do not all need to be answered:

1. What would your reaction be?
2. How would you feel about leaving your country, your people, and your parents' household?
3. What would this mean to you?
4. What would you miss?
5. What would you be glad to leave?
6. What would you take with you? Leave behind?
7. What would you say to God? Why?
8. How do you feel about becoming a great nation, having a great name, being blessed by God, receiving land?
9. How do you feel about being a blessing to others? What does this mean to you?

 Focus Questions

1. Is God's calling of the Adventist Church conditional or unconditional?
2. A covenant is an agreement. How does God make agreements with us today?
3. How do we know God's call and will for our lives?
4. How does your mission in life correspond with that of the church?

FAITH

I seek not for a faith that will move a mountain, but for a faith that will somehow move me (Unknown).

Abraham: His Faith and Fears

Lesson Scripture: Genesis 12:8, 20, 21

Faith is like a kiss. Though you may talk about a kiss, analyze it, define it, and even practice "lip-ups" on the mirror, it is not a kiss until you experience it by kissing someone else. So it is with faith. For faith needs to be experienced to be genuine. Abraham experienced genuine faith in his life, as recorded in Hebrews 11:8-17:

- "By faith Abraham, when called to go to a place . . . , obeyed and went, even though he did not know where he was going."
- "By faith Abraham, even though he was past age . . . was enabled to become a father."
- "By faith Abraham, when

God tested him, offered Isaac as a sacrifice."

But what is faith? Is it an ability, a commodity, an attitude, a belief, or a behavior? In this lesson, we will examine the biblical concept of faith.

DEFINING FAITH

Faith involves both a concept and an action. It is a belief or mental conviction that leads to an action of confidence toward an object.

Faith is a key term in the Bible. However, there is only one text that defines faith—Hebrews 11:1. Note how the following versions render this passage:

- "Now faith is the *substance of things* hoped for, the *evidence of things* not seen" (KJV).

- "Now faith is *being sure* of what we hope for and *certain* of what we do not see" (NIV).
- "Now faith is the *assurance of things* hoped for, the *conviction of things* not seen" (RSV).
- "Now faith means *full confidence* in the things we hope for, it means being *certain* of things we cannot see" (Phillips).

These versions explain faith as the "substance of things," "evidence of things," "being sure," "certain," "assurance of things," "the conviction of things," "full confidence." In summary, faith is an internal confidence in obtaining something not yet received.

However, this is only the theoretical part of faith's definition. The rest of the definition is given in verses 4 to 39, "By faith . . ." the biblical heroes acted. This abstract mental confidence became an active part of their lives. These heroes of Hebrews 11 were willing to take risks to do what God wanted. For example, "By faith Abraham, when called to go to a place he would later receive as his inheritance, obeyed and went, even though he did not know where he was going" (verse 8, NIV). "You see that his faith and his actions were working together, and his faith was made complete by what he did" (James 2:22, NIV).

SOURCE OF FAITH

Where does this kind of faith come from? Is it inherited, or is it acquired? According to the Bible, every person is given a measure of faith. This kind of faith is called "your faith." As in "your faith has made you whole." This faith is a gift from God and one of the fruits of the Spirit. It can be increased or decreased depending on how a person responds to hearing God's Word. However, the primary source of faith is Jesus, "the author and perfector of our faith" (Hebrews 12:2, NIV).

OBJECT OF FAITH

What makes faith genuine is its object. Whether you are examining the lives of the biblical heroes or reading their writings, their faith has only one object, Jesus Christ. The key is not the greatness of your faith but the greatness of the One in whom you have faith. David sings, "He is my refuge and my

fortress, my God, in whom I trust" (Psalm 91:2, NIV). John observes, "This is his command: to believe in the name of his Son, Jesus Christ" (1 John 3:23, NIV). Paul proclaims, "I am not ashamed of the gospel, because it is the power of God for the salvation of everyone who believes" (Romans 1:16, NIV).

Let's return to Abraham. Paul uses this man's faith as an example of a Christ-centered faith. "Consider Abraham: 'He believed God, and it was credited to him as righteousness.' Understand, then, that those who believe are children of Abraham. The Scripture foresaw that God would justify the Gentiles by faith, and announced the gospel in advance to Abraham: 'All nations will be blessed through you.' . . . You are all sons of God through faith in Christ Jesus. . . . If you belong to Christ, then you are Abraham's seed, and heirs according to the promise" (Galatians 3:6-9, 26, 29, NIV).

FIGHTING THE GOOD FIGHT

Spiritual faith is the biblical term for a confidence we have about something we possess in Christ but don't yet see in ourselves. It becomes the basis for our actions in life. This kind of faith comes from God and finds its confidence in Christ's victory over sin for us. Peter summarizes this by saying, "Though you have not seen him, you love him; and even though you do not see him now, you believe in him and are filled with an inexpressible and glorious joy, for you are receiving the goal of your faith, the salvation of your souls" (1 Peter 1:8, 9, NIV).

Paul advises us to "fight the good fight of faith." But what is this good fight of faith? It is the fight to make Jesus our Saviour and the supreme aim of life. It is the struggle to put Jesus in the center of our activity. Forever remaining and trusting in Jesus. "By faith Abraham . . ."

Memory Focus

. . . .

 # Into the Bible

1. Examine the following passages in Genesis, and identify two examples in each passage of Abraham's faith and trust in God:

   A. 12:4-8   C. 18:19, 22-28
   B. 14:13-24   D. 22:1-11

2. Examine the following passages in Genesis, and identify two examples in each passage of Abraham's doubts and failures:

   A. 12:10-13   C. 16:1-5
   B. 15:1, 2, 8   D. 17:17, 18

3. Abraham struggled with issues that are still common today. Read the following passages in Genesis to see how Abraham succeeded or failed in his handling of the issues. From each passage, list two principles we can use when faced with the same or similar issue:

   A. 12:10-13—Dealing with a crisis.
   B. 13:5-9—Managing personal and civil rights.
   C. 14:13-24—Coping with political problems.
   D. 16:1-5—Struggling with sexual and family pressures.
   E. 18:1-8—Offering hospitality (homelessness and hunger).
   F. 20:1, 2, 11-13—Treating a loved one.

4. In Romans 4:1-3, Paul explains that Abraham was justified by faith apart from works. With this in mind, read James 2:14-24, which seems to indicate that Abraham was justified by both faith and works. After reading James 2:14-24, complete the following activities:

   A. Write out three key passages that reveal the relationship

between faith and works.

    B. In your own words, explain the illustration given in verses 15 and 16.

    C. In the sequence of Abraham's life, which came first, his faith or the offering of Isaac?

    D. Write your definition of faith, showing the relationship between faith and works.

Projects

1. MAGIC SQUARE: Obtain a copy of the activity "Magic Square" from your teacher. Complete the Magic Square by following the instructions on the sheet.

2. SOURCE OF FAITH: Write a short paragraph explaining the source of faith. Use the following texts as resources:

   2 Peter 1:2; Hebrews 11:1, 4; 12:2; Ephesians 1:13; 2:8; Romans 10:17; 12:3; Acts 3:16; 4:4; John 1:7; 20:29.

3. Devise a plan that would allow your faith in Christ to be tested and grow within the setting of your school. Keep a diary of the experience, and give a report to the class.

4. Use the Canaan outline map supplied by your teacher to identify the geographic locations listed on the instruction sheet.

Focus Questions

1. Can one be faithless?
2. What relationship does the faith humans have in each other have with saving faith in Christ?
3. What are the similarities and differences between a "daredevil" and a "faith taker"?
4. What is the meaning of the quote "The life is molded by the faith" (*The Great Controversy*, 597)? Do you agree or disagree with it?
5. How could Abraham be called the "father of the faithful" (Romans 4:11), when at times he showed a lack of faith?

DEVOTION

When God measures the greatness of an individual, He puts the tape measure around the heart, not the head *(Quips and Quotes)*.

lesson 22

Abraham: His Son and Sacrifice

Lesson Scripture: Genesis 22:1-18

In our Western culture, the names we're given at birth don't have much meaning. Oh, they may mean a lot to a parent or grandparent, if we happen to be named after one of them. And now and then, a child is given the name of a particular thing, such as Rock or April. But most of the time, names are just something to call people, like Bob or Jane. The only way to find out if they mean something else is to check a dictionary of names, where long ago in the forgotten past you might find your name once meant "intelligent" or "spear carrier."

But this is not true of all cultures. In many parts of the world, names have a natural meaning recognizable to any-one who hears them. You probably have heard the descriptive Native American names Sitting Bull and Crazy Horse, to give just two examples.

In biblical times, people were often given names that described some aspect of their character or appearance. But these meanings have become obscure to modern readers of the Bible. For example, we know certain Old Testament characters today as Abraham, Isaac, Jacob, and Esau. To us, these are just names. But when these men were alive, their names told a great deal about them.

Take the twin brothers Jacob and Esau. In Hebrew, *Esau* means "hairy," and indeed, the Bible says Esau was rather bearlike in that regard. *Jacob* means "grabber," which may seem strange until we remem-

ber that Jacob was born holding his brother's heel. Later, he grabbed Esau's inheritance out from under him. Jacob lived with that unfortunate name until one night he wrestled with an angel. After that, God decided a better name for Jacob would be Israel, which means in Hebrew "one who prevails with God." I'm sure Jacob approved of the change.

ABRAHAM'S NEW NAME

What does all this have to do with Abraham, his son Isaac, and that terrible day when Abraham nearly killed his son on an altar of stones? Just this. Isaac and Abraham also had names with particular meaning in the Hebrew language, and knowing the story of their names can give us insight into the strange, disturbing tale of their experience on Mount Moriah.

Isaac's name meant "laughter." And the meaning of that name is all bound up in the story of how he came to be born at all.

When Isaac's father was ninety-nine years old, God changed his name from *Abram*, meaning "exalted father," to *Abraham*, meaning "father of a multitude." There was just one problem: Abraham was nobody's father, and at his age, the possibility of ever being a father was remote indeed. Abraham may have clung to the hope embodied in his new name for a long time. But as year after year passed with no offspring, that name must have seemed like a cruel joke.

God had promised Abraham that his descendants would be a multitude too numerous to count. But when it seemed that God was not following through on that promise, Abraham and his wife Sarah (her name meant "princess") decided to take matters into their own hands. Perhaps the problem, they thought, was that Sarah was too old to bear children. After all, the promise concerned Abraham's children, not necessarily hers. So she suggested an alternate plan: Abraham could have a child with her maid Hagar.

But God has ways of letting us know when He requires our help to carry out His plans. And when He doesn't, we would be wise to let Him work things out in His own time. The people who built the Tower of Babel learned this lesson the hard way, and now Abraham and Sarah had fallen into the same trap.

Hagar did conceive a child with Abraham, but things didn't turn out happily. In Hebrew, *Hagar* means "flight," and before her child was born, Hagar was forced to flee into the desert to escape Sarah's jealous anger. God watched over Hagar in her flight and assured her that even though others had rejected her, He had heard her cries and would make her son great. God told Hagar to name the boy Ishmael, which means "God hears," as a reminder of His mercy.

Meanwhile, God had not forgotten His promise to Abraham. He was well aware that Sarah was too old to have children. But after they had tried to work things out their own way, He stepped in with His supernatural plan. Sarah did conceive and did give birth to a son, fourteen years after the birth of Ishmael had brought anger and separation to their family. They named the boy Isaac, meaning "laughter," as a reminder of how Sarah had laughed out loud at the thought of bearing a child at her age. God had taken her by surprise after a lifetime of waiting. And now Isaac was the first member of the promised multitude.

ABRAHAM'S TERRIBLE TEST

Twenty years later, Isaac was a grown man, Abraham was a rich man, and there was every reason to believe that God would carry out His promise to make Abraham and his family a great nation.

Then, out of the blue, the promise seemed in peril once again—and for the most incredible reason! One night, Abraham awoke after hearing the unmistakable voice of God telling him to take Isaac to the land of Moriah and sacrifice him as a burnt offering. For twenty years, Abraham had lived, as all fathers do, in terror of losing his son through an accident or illness. But he had never imagined this!

He left his tent and went out into the night to clear his head. He looked up into the desert sky, brilliant with a host of stars. He remembered God's promise to make his descendants just as numerous as the stars and was tempted to think he had just had a bad dream. He prayed for guidance, but the only answer was, "Take your son, your only son, Isaac, whom you love" (Genesis 22:2, NIV).

In the next three days, Abraham took the longest

203

journey of his life. He didn't tell Sarah or Isaac about the voice in the night or about what he planned to do on Moriah. Isaac would have to be told soon enough, but what would he tell Sarah when he came home alone? Three days of agony. Three days of silent prayer. Three days for Satan to tempt him to once again take matters into his own hands. But this was a new Abraham, who no longer relied on himself to fulfill God's purposes. God's overwhelming goodness in giving him Isaac had made his faith rock solid. Isaac himself was a miracle, Knowing that prepared Abraham to face this test of faith. Isaac's birth was a miracle, and God could resurrect him.

When they reached the foot of Mount Moriah, Abraham dismissed the servants. He and Isaac went on alone, Isaac carrying the wood, Abraham the knife and fire.

Somewhere near the top, Isaac found the courage to ask his father the question that had been nagging him for some time. "I see the fire and the wood, but where is the lamb?"

All his grief-stricken father could say was, "God Himself will provide the lamb."

Together they built the altar and arranged the wood. Then, with words that must have nearly choked him, Abraham revealed the secret of God's command. What must Isaac have felt? Terror at the thought of such a death? Awed that God had chosen him for this special purpose? We do know that he didn't run or try to overpower his father. He offered no resistance, confident that God's way is always best.

This is one of those wonderful stories in which joy is snatched from the clutches of tragedy at the very last moment. But that last moment was time enough. As Abraham lifted the knife, a heavenly voice called out, "Abraham! Abraham!"

"Here I am," he replied.

"Do not lay a hand on the boy," he said. "Do not do anything to him. Now I know that you fear God, because you have not withheld from me your son, your only son" (Genesis 22:11, 12, NIV).

God led Abraham to a ram caught in a bush by its horns. The ram took Isaac's place on the altar of offering, and the story ends with yet another name. With joy and gratitude, Abraham named the place of sacrifice Jehovah-jireh, which means "the Lord will provide." ⚲

 # Memory Focus

"Consider Abraham: 'He believed God, and it was credited to him as righteousness' " (Galatians 3:6, NIV).

OR

"The next day John saw Jesus coming toward him and said, 'Look, the Lamb of God, who takes away the sin of the world' " (John 1:29, NIV)!

 # Into the Bible

1. The term *righteousness by faith* or *justification by faith* is first used in the story of Abraham. Abraham is an example of those who are declared righteous by faith. To better understand what this means and its importance to your salvation, do the following: Consult a Bible dictionary, and write out the definitions for *righteousness* and *justification.*

2. Read Romans 4:18-25, and answer the following questions:

   A. What did Abraham do that showed great faith?
   B. What does this have to do with how you are saved?

3. What parallels do you see between the story of Abraham sacrificing Isaac and our salvation? Read the following texts: 1 Corinthians 15:3; 2 Corinthians 5:14, 21; 1 John 4:10; and find the answers to the questions.

   A. Whom does Isaac represent?
   B. Whom does Abraham represent?
   C. Whom does the ram represent?

4. Isaac was rescued from his death penalty. How can we escape ours? Read John 1:12; 1 Peter 1:18, 19; 2:24; 3:18 to find how we can escape our death penalty.

5. According to Hebrews 11:17-19, what did Abraham believe God would do for them on Mt. Moriah?

 **Projects**

1. Imagine you are one of the following characters. Write a letter to your best friend describing the events that occurred on Mount Moriah.
    *   Abraham
    *   Sarah
    *   Isaac
    *   One of the servants on the trip to the mountain.
2. Read *Patriarchs and Prophets*, pages 145-155. Then write a letter to your best friend as if you were one of the following characters:
    *   Abraham
    *   Sarah
    *   Isaac
    *   One of Abraham's servants accompanying him on a trip
3. Read *Patriarchs and Prophets*, pages 145-155, and answer the following questions:

    A. What gave Abraham the strength and courage to go through with God's command to offer his son Isaac?
    B. How was the "gospel" presented on Mount Moriah? You should compare and contrast the "ram caught in the thicket" on Mount Moriah and the fact that there was no "ram in the thicket" on Mt. Calvary.
    C. Write a paragraph explaining what you think is the most important lesson one should learn from this event on Mount Moriah.

 **Focus Questions**

1. If God is all-knowing, then He must have known how Abraham would respond to His test. Why did He need to give the test anyway?

2. Does God ever need our "help" to accomplish His plans?
3. Does God really "help those who help themselves"? Sometimes? Always? Never?
4. What can we learn from the fact that Isaac didn't run away from his fate?
5. Can you think of other parallels between Christ and Isaac besides the fact that they were both sacrifices? Hints: (1) their unusual births, (2) they each carried something to the place of their deaths, (3) the outcome of their "deaths."
6. Abraham did not rely on faith when he fathered Ishmael. So is it fair that Paul should refer to him as an example of righteousness by faith?
7. Does knowing that Jesus was the sacrifice for your sins have a direct effect on your thinking or behavior? How?
8. What did the angel do for Isaac that angels couldn't do for Jesus on the cross?
9. After reading the story of Abraham and Isaac, can you give a definition of "sacrifice" in your own words?
10. In what ways does Abraham illustrate God the Father in the plan of salvation?

unit 4

God, You, and Your Family

Abraham to Joseph

Unit four emphasizes God's love and concern for His people and the divine characteristics of love, compassion, and forgiveness. The contrast of tragic consequences for spiritual failures with the impact of joyful rewards for faithfulness in following God's principles is revealed in the stories of Lot and Joseph.

There are modern-day applications of biblical principles to lifestyle issues. Priorities, values, and standards for relationships within and outside the family are emphasized.

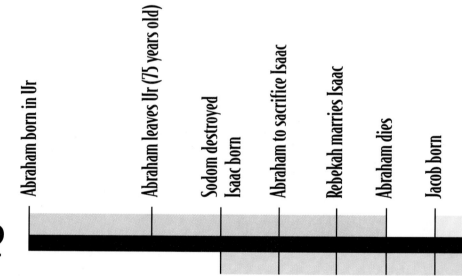

Time

Abraham born in Ur

Abraham leaves Ur (75 years old)

Sodom destroyed
Isaac born

Abraham to sacrifice Isaac

Rebekah marries Isaac

Abraham dies

Jacob born

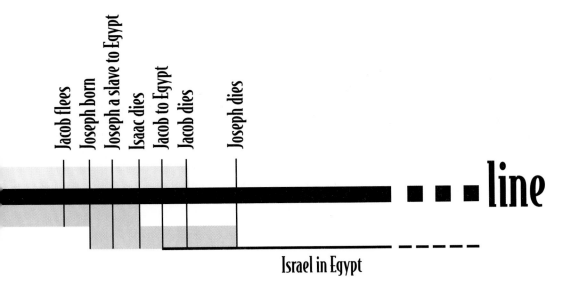

Jacob flees
Joseph born
Joseph a slave to Egypt
Isaac dies
Jacob to Egypt
Jacob dies
Joseph dies

line

Israel in Egypt

FOCUS

Aim at heaven, and you'll get earth thrown in. Aim at earth, and you'll get neither *(C.S. Lewis)*.

lesson 23

Escape From the City Sin Destroyed

Lesson Scripture: Genesis 19:1-29

**W**hat's the most fun you ever had on a trip to a big city?

Was it the time your family took a sports vacation? A basketball game with the Bulls in Chicago. Baseball at Fenway Park in Boston. Hockey in Montreal. Football in Miami. The Olympics in Atlanta.

Or was it your class trip to the Smithsonian museums in Washington, D.C.? Air and Space. Natural History. American History. Art. Even the National Zoo.

Or the time you took in all the entertainment possibilities around LA? The original Disneyland. Knott's Berry Farm. The Rose Parade.

Of course, you can't forget the time you ate at those incredible restaurants in New Orleans. Especially that outdoor cafe, right next to the river, that served delicious pastries with powdered sugar and hot chocolate.

Or the time you stood in the gallery of the New York Stock Exchange and realized how many millions of dollars were changing hands right before your eyes.

And how about that beautiful night you stood at the top of Lombard Street in San Francisco and looked across the city lights to the Golden Gate Bridge?

A CITY LIKE THE GARDEN OF EDEN

Cities can be wonderful, exciting places, can't they?

That's the kind of city Sodom was. Listen to this description from the book *Patriarchs and Prophets*, pages 156-158. "Fairest among the cities of the Jordan Valley was Sodom, set in a plain which was 'as the garden of the Lord' in its fertility and beauty. . . . Art and commerce combined to enrich the proud city of the plain. The treasures of the East adorned her palaces, and the caravans of the desert brought their stores of precious things to supply her marts of trade. With little thought or labor, every want of life could be supplied, and the whole year seemed one round of festivity. . . . Evening fell upon a scene of loveliness and security. A landscape of unrivaled beauty. . . . The coolness of eventide . . . the enjoyment of the hour."

THE DARK SIDE OF CITIES

But there's another side to cities. Beneath the glamour, behind the mask of pleasure, around the corner and down the alleys is a hellish nightmare of pain and despair. Homeless people prowling in garbage dumpsters for food. Out-of-control mobs breaking windows, setting fires, overturning parked cars, beating up innocent passersby. Drug dealers. Prostitutes. Violent crime. Unbelievable poverty. Open defiance of the law.

Sodom was like *that* too.

"They defaced the image of God, and became satanic. . . . The vilest and most brutal passions were unrestrained. The people openly defied God and His law and delighted in deeds of violence" (*Patriarchs and Prophets*, 156, 157).

How can beautiful, caring people, created in the image of God, become satanic? What influences promote such a transformation? Before you continue with this lesson, take a few moments to write down three actions you think reveal Satan's influence. Then try to identify the smaller steps people take down the road to that satanic end.

JUST ANOTHER DAY IN THE CITY

It had been another scorching day. But now the evening breezes were cooling the city streets. Crowds were already gathering at the finer restaurants and the most outrageous theaters. Tourists were searching for hotels. Gangs of young men were scouting out their territory. A lot of people were already drunk.

In the twilight, two men appeared at the gate of the city. Unhurried, calm, assured, they walked toward the center of town as if they knew just where they were going and exactly what they were about to do.

Lot had never seen either of these two men before. Knowing the abuse to which strangers in Sodom were exposed, Lot had made it his responsibility to get visitors off the street before the worst happened. Lot moved quickly but stealthily. The last thing he wanted to do was draw attention.

"Excuse me, sirs," Lot said as he stepped in front of the men. "I couldn't help but notice you're new in town. No doubt you need a place to spend the night. I'd like to offer you a room in my home."

Lot wasn't surprised by the men's quick refusal. Sodom had a well-deserved reputation. Thousands of mothers had warned their sons never to talk to strangers, especially men from Sodom. "No, thank you," the men replied. "We're just planning to spend the night somewhere out here on the street."

Lot was astounded. *They don't know,* he thought to himself. *They're ignorant. Or from another country.*

"No, I insist," pressed Lot. "It would be unthinkable and inhospitable. Please, let me offer you entertainment at my place."

The men finally accepted, and the rest, as they say, is history. The gathering of the noisy, lawless crowd. The brutal intentions. Lot's desperate pleas. The narrow escape. The sudden blindness. The angels revealing themselves and their mission. The family laughing about any possible danger.

AN UNEXPECTED DETOUR

Early the next morning, the angels took Lot, his wife, and two daughters by the hand and pulled them out of their luxurious home. In the predawn dimness, they quickly moved down the main street of town and out of the city. Only then did the angels loosen their grip.

"Keep moving toward the mountains," the angels warned. Then the two messengers turned silently toward Sodom and walked back to complete the task that had brought them to this place (see *Patriarchs and Prophets*, 160).

But the family didn't listen to the angels. They slowed their pace and began thinking about their friends still in the city. And the beautiful home they were leaving behind. And all the years of hard work for the people of Sodom.

Suddenly another person was standing beside them, urging them to hurry, to escape to the mountains before the destruction took place. It was Jesus, Creator, Protector. The Prince of Heaven. Nothing in the universe was more important on this morning than these four citizens of Sodom walking across the plain toward the distant mountains.

In their confused and earthbound perspective, the family members did not recognize who it was who was urging them on. Instead, Lot allowed his fears to overpower him.

"We'll never make it," he gasped. "The mountains are too far away, and we're already out of breath."

"Hurry," Jesus said. "Leave the city behind."

"Perhaps we should have stayed in Sodom. Maybe we could have talked the angels out of their plans."

"Don't stop now. You're almost safe."

"If we had a few more days, we probably could have convinced others to come with us."

"You've done all you can do for the others. Keep walking."

"I've got an idea. There's a little town just at the foot of the hills. It's called Zoar. Maybe we should stop there in case there's something we can do back in Sodom tomorrow."

"All right," Jesus said patiently. "Stop in Zoar. I won't destroy it. But there won't be any tomorrow in Sodom."

Lot and his daughters turned off the main road and headed down the path to Zoar.

Lot's wife had already turned back toward Sodom. She stood still now, her form frozen in the direction of where her heart remained.

THUNDER FROM AN UNCLOUDED SKY

Lot and his daughters had been in Zoar for only seconds when they heard the explosion, felt the shock waves, and saw the fire reflected in the eyes of the people.

"Suddenly and unexpectedly as would be a thunder peal from an unclouded sky, the tempest broke. The Lord rained brimstone and fire out of heaven upon the cities and the fruitful plain" (*Patriarchs and Prophets*, 162). Everything was consumed. The palaces and temples. The expensive homes. The gardens and vineyards. And most sadly, the people. All the people. The destruction was complete. The smoke continued to rise for days. Nothing survived.

Nothing ever lived in Sodom again. 🚶

Memory Focus

"Clothe yourselves with the Lord Jesus Christ, and do not think about how to gratify the desires of the sinful nature" (Romans 13:14, NIV).

OR

"The grace of God that brings salvation has appeared to all men. It teaches us to say 'No' to ungodliness and worldly passions, and to live self-controlled, upright and godly lives in this present age" (Titus 2:11, 12, NIV).

· ·

Into the Bible

1. A. Summarize what the Bible says regarding the practice of homosexuality.

    (1) Leviticus 18:22
    (2) Romans 1:26-28
    (3) 1 Corinthians 6:9, 10

    B. In light of Lot's experiences in Sodom, consider what is said in Ezekiel 16:48-50. Make a list of the social ills for which God rebuked Sodom and Gomorrah that are still present in our day.

    C. Describe the counsel Scripture gives Christian believers regarding their moral conduct.

    (1) 1 Thessalonians 4:3-7
    (2) Galatians 5:19-21
    (3) 1 Corinthians 6:18-20

2. The beings who visited Abraham and Lot were angels sent on a special mission to communicate with humans. Read the following biblical passages that describe the work of angels. Share your findings in class, and discuss the ways in which angels have interacted with human beings.

A. Their mission to God's people: Psalm 34:7; Hebrews 1:14.
B. The mission to Balaam: Numbers 22:22-35.
C. The deliverance of Daniel: Daniel 6:21, 22.
D. Ministering to Jesus: Matthew 4:11; 28:2; Luke 24:4-7.

3. Occasionally, in biblical history, there are stories of a loving God *destroying* instead of giving life. In Sodom, all the inhabitants of the city, as well as Lot's wife, experienced the execution of God's judgment.

   Read the stories in the passages listed below. Then write a paragraph that identifies the following: (A) common themes, (B) how the passages harmonize God's justice with His love.

   - The Flood: Genesis 6:5-8.
   - The Assyrian army: 2 Kings 19:9-19, 35, 36.
   - Ananias and Sapphira: Acts 5:1-11.
   - The final act of destruction: Revelation 20:7-9.

 # Projects

1. Take a closer look at the life of Lot. The Bible record provides clues about Lot's character that help us see that he was heading for trouble. Examine the passages below that tell the story of three episodes in the lives of Abraham and Lot. Then write a couple of sentences that contrast Abraham's principles with Lot's.

   A. Choosing where to live: Genesis 13:1-13.
   B. Prisoner of war: Genesis 14:1-24.
   C. Priorities: Genesis 18:16-33 and 19:1-11.

2. In the Bible, cities are used as illustrations of God's kingdom and as illustrations of the kingdom of evil. Using the texts on the worksheet your teacher will provide, select passages in which the word *city* (or name of a city) stands for positive principles. Then select those that are referred to in a negative way. Also identify the characteristics that determine if a city is used to illustrate good or evil.

3. How does God feel about homosexual *people?* Why is it more

3. How does God feel about homosexual *people?* Why is it more difficult for us to separate our feelings about certain actions from our reactions to certain people? Why is it so easy to equate the sin with the sinner? This project deals with the difficult subject of how Christians should treat homosexuals. Just to be sure that God doesn't expect us to act more kindly than He is willing to act, look up the passages in the following chart, and write a summary for each.

The Commandment	The Sin	God's Relationship to the Sinner
A. Exodus 20:16	Genesis 12:10-20	James 2:23
B. Exodus 20:13	Exodus 2:11, 12	Exodus 33:11
C. 1 Cor. 6:15	Joshua 2:1	Matt. 1:5
		Heb. 11:31
D. Deut. 21:8, 9	Acts 8:3; 9:1	Acts 9:15-17

4. Look at each of the statements below that describe possible actions people might take toward homosexuals. Find a story in a newspaper or newsmagazine that supports the statement below that best reflects your position regarding homosexuality. Explain how the story or article represents your position.

   A. *Gay Bashing.* It doesn't bother me when homosexuals are beaten.
   B. *Verbal Harassment.* I would be comfortable verbally taunting a gay person.
   C. *Legal Discrimination.* I support making clear distinctions based on sexual preference.
   D. *Legal Protection.* I believe all forms of discrimination should be illegal.
   E. *Room for Friendship.* I would be comfortable having a gay person for a friend.
   F. *Lifestyle Acceptance.* I don't think gay people should be expected to change their lifestyle.

 **Focus Questions**

1. Why do we have a responsibility to the needy? Have you done anything to help the homeless, feed the hungry, and bring hope to discouraged people?
2. What are the little steps that ultimately lead people to satanic ends? How can you avoid that process in your own life?
3. Why do you think the angels did not reveal their mission to Lot immediately?
4. What part did Lot play in the death of his wife?
5. How can we better understand the execution of God's judgment? See Psalm 73 for one response.
6. As you examine your own attitude toward homosexuals, how can you demonstrate God's love for sinners and His condemnation of sin?
7. Since the Bible condemns homosexuality, is it intolerant to say it is wrong?
8. Is AIDS a divine judgment on sexually immoral people?
9. If a member of your church had AIDS, how would you react or relate to him/her?

REFLECTED GLORY
The world doesn't need a definition of religion as much as it needs a demonstration *(Quips and Quotes)*.

Reflecting God's Glory

**Lesson Scriptures: Romans 12:1, 2;
1 Corinthians 6:12; Romans 14:8-13;
Romans 2:1-4; 1 Peter 2:1-16**

I was the guest preacher at a church many miles from home. For my Sabbath sermon, I used texts from Romans and Galatians to describe how God is head-over-heels in love with us. I focused on God's salvation that He so freely offers to everyone. I shared how God loves sinners so much that He offers them total acceptance in Christ the moment they receive Him as their Saviour and Lord. And with this acceptance comes forgiveness. And transformation.

The congregation listened intently and seemed moved by the glory of God's grace. I met many new friends at the church door, shook a hundred hands, and then followed the crowd to the fellowship hall.

The potluck was excellent. One of the potato salad dishes had been made without onions, there were two kinds of home-made dill pickles, and someone had even provided pecan pie for dessert.

During the meal, I sat across from a very happy young woman. I remember her smile, her earrings, and her story. I'm learning to look directly into eyes and purposefully ignore ear lobes, necks, and any jewelry that may be hanging there. But this time the jewelry was too beautiful and large to ignore. The earrings were turquoise and silver, obviously crafted by a talented artisan. In fact, the artist had taken a series of black lines in the stones and carried the design on out into the silver, creating a stylized picture of Kokopelli, the Navajo flute player. They were exquisite!

"Do you have some Navajo friends?" I tried not to look at her ears.

"Oh." Her smile grew even brighter. "You noticed my earrings! Aren't they wonderful!" For the next ten minutes, we talked about her Navajo friends, her trips to the reservation, and the talented artist who had made the earrings especially for her. We also talked about her relationship with Christ.

"Last Sabbath was the happiest day of my life!" Her smile placed dozens of exclamation points around her words. "Last Sabbath I was baptized right here in the church. Now I'm a Seventh-day Adventist, and it's the best thing that has ever happened to me. Isn't it wonderful to be in love with Jesus!"

For a brief moment, I wondered if her earrings had been baptized too. But I pushed that thought aside and continued the warm fellowship with my new friend.

As I was getting into my car for the trip home, the pastor's wife came walking slowly across the parking lot. I rolled down the window and told her how much I had enjoyed visiting their congregation. She leaned down, cleared her throat, frowned, and asked the question that had obviously been tormenting her all morning.

"If I agree with what you said about God accepting sinners, about God liking people who are still doing sinful things, then what is the reason for all of the Adventist standards?"

"What specifically concerns you?" I asked.

She leaned almost into the car, pausing. Her reply was obviously genuine and filled with sincere hope for a useful answer. "How do I get the earrings off the new members?"

I imagined a confrontation between this earnest pastor's wife and the joyful new member with the turquoise earrings. I heard words about "Christian lifestyle" and the need to stand out from the world. I saw hands reaching out to remove the offending objects. As the scene faded from my mind, I asked, "Would this improve her spiritual experience? Would keeping them on be a hindrance?"

She hadn't thought of it that way before. I waited as her eyes looked up toward the sky, focused on an invisible cloud, and imagined the possibilities.

Her response was slow, thoughtful, and wonderfully

honest. "No. I don't suppose removing them would improve *her* spiritual experience. But it would improve *mine!*"

Then her eyes looked on mine, and I could see the confusion and frustration welling up. "It was all so easy when everything was black and white. Now everything seems to be just shades of gray."

In each Seventh-day Adventist congregation, there are differing convictions about the Adventist lifestyle. Some members believe certain behaviors are unacceptable for an Adventist. Others look at the same behaviors and do not see any issue of morality. It is possible that our lifestyle disagreements will pull us farther and farther apart. It is also possible (and preferable) that these disagreements will bring us back to the Scriptures with a united desire to find God's answers and a respectful tolerance for different conclusions.

These issues are especially significant to teenagers, who by nature question and test boundaries. Adventist teens often focus their testing on these lifestyle standards. This can bring frustration and worry to the older members with each new challenge on the accepted

way of living. In early Adventism, the questions were about purchasing bicycles, wearing hoop skirts, and playing tennis. Later, questions relating to standards moved to the playing of chess, going to movies, the reading of fiction, and whether women could wear pants or miniskirts and still be good Adventists.

Sometimes we focus on the behaviors themselves rather than the reasons for choosing such behaviors. Standards of conduct and lifestyle are upheld while appropriate reasons and motivations are too often overlooked. The issue of lifestyle standards has two important sides—the need for valid reasons and the need for a willing, accepting spirit. Morality is concerned primarily with right behavior, but Christianity views conduct in the light of one's

relationships and inner attitude.

Youth have often tested, questioned, and pushed the limits. But now, they don't only ask, "Is it right?" or "What's wrong with . . . ?" Today's youth also ask, "What does this have to do with me?" and "Why is this a big deal?" Meaning and personal relevance are as important as the behavior itself.

As Christians, our lifestyle choices are rooted in three essential facts about our existence.

1. Sin is a fatal rebellion that separates us from God.
2. Christ has opened the way back to God by dying in our place for our sins and then rising, victorious, from the tomb.
3. God offers this salvation as a gift to anyone who receives Jesus as Lord.

There are two great enemies of this grace. One is open rebellion against God and an unwillingness to do His will. The other is a rigid, legalistic religion that reduces holiness to a list of correct behaviors. Both distortions are deadly. So what does it mean to be an authentic, effective disciple of Christ?

My family (which includes three teenagers) have been thinking about all of this for the past many months. We haven't discovered any final answers or perfect solutions, but we have developed two sets of principles that help us make decisions about most lifestyle issues. You may find these principles helpful as you debate what you watch, what you wear, what you eat and what you drink, what books you read, and how you spend your Saturday nights.

UNIVERSAL LIFESTYLE PRINCIPLES

1. 1 Peter 2:16; Galatians 5:1, 13.
   The principle of freedom.
   Christ has set me free from serving self to follow Him.

2. Colossians 3:10; 1 Peter 2:11, 12.
   The principle of responsibility.
   Christ calls me to use my freedom to serve others in love.

FIVE PRINCIPLES OF EVALUATION FOR LIFESTYLE CHOICES

1. Hebrews 12:1, 2.
   Excess.
   Could this slow me down spiritually?

2. 1 Corinthians 6:12a.
   Experience.
   Is this profitable and useful
   in my life plan?

3. Galatians 5:19-25.
   Enslavement.
   Will this allow me to be
   Spirit-controlled?

4. Romans 14:7, 8.
   Example.
   Can I be a good example to
   others?

5. 1 Corinthians 9:19.
   Evangelism.
   Does it enable me to win
   others to Christ? 🏃

. . . .

💿 Memory Focus

"Dear friends, I urge you, as aliens and strangers in the world, to abstain from sinful desires, which war against your soul. Live such good lives among the pagans that, though they accuse you of doing wrong, they may see your good deeds and glorify God on the day he visits us" (1 Peter 2:11, 12, NIV).

OR

"Friends, this world is not your home, so don't make yourselves cozy in it. Don't indulge your ego at the expense of your soul. Live an exemplary life among the natives so that your actions will refute their prejudices. Then they'll be won over to God's side and be there to join in the celebration when he arrives" (1 Peter 2:11, 12, The Message).

OR

"When the nations are gathered before Him, there will be but two classes, and their eternal destiny will be determined by what they have done or neglected to do for Him in the person of the poor and suffering" (*The Desire of Ages*, 637).

 Into the Bible

1. Create a list of five lifestyle issues in your home, church, or school. On the worksheet provided by your teacher, you will do the following regarding these:
   Select two issues from the list and . . .

   - . . . identify the key word of each of the five principles of evaluation.
   - . . . describe how each of the principles applies to the issue.
   - . . . write a summary paragraph explaining your personal convictions about each of the two issues.

2. In the narrative, the pastor's wife expressed the concern that someone else's behavior could affect her spiritual growth. In other words, Christian freedom must be considered in the light of our Christian influence. Since our lifestyle behaviors reveal our values and priorities, these behaviors greatly affect other people. A challenge for each Christian is working through the process of applying the principles of our faith to what we wear, how we act, what we do, and so much more.

   A. Read the following texts, and write a sentence that summarizes what each passage says about our freedom and influence.

   - John 8:32
   - Romans 14:12, 13
   - 1 Corinthians 8:9, 13
   - 2 Corinthians 3:17, 18
   - Galatians 5:13-18
   - 1 Peter 2:11-17

   B. Stretch your creativity! Create a poem, draw a picture, write a song, or write a two- to three-minute speech to present to the class expressing the relationship between one's freedom and influence.

3. As a person takes off dirty clothes and puts on clean ones, likewise, the Christian renounces sinful ways and chooses a new kind of life. Colossians 3 describes the needed changes that take place in our walk with the Lord.

   A. Read Colossians 3:5-14. Make two lists of traits or behaviors that one adopts as a growing Christian. Label one list "What comes off," and label the other list "What is put on."

   B. Our Christian journey includes the daily struggle of change. Throughout this experience, according to Colossians 3:1-4, explain what provides power and assurance for change.

. . . .

 Projects

1. A. Rate the following activities according to the five principles of evaluation listed in the narrative:

   (1) Picking up around an old person's home.
   (2) Attending a hockey game.
   (3) Tutoring elementary-school children.
   (4) Offering free baby-sitting to families who need to get away.
   (5) Watching MTV with your friends.
   (6) Working one evening a week in a homeless feeding center.
   (7) Playing popular video games.
   (8) Helping the Community Service center prepare disaster supplies.
   (9) Raising money for a family who cannot pay their power bill.
   (10) Attending a Christian rock concert.

   B. Now, add three of your own activities, and rate them.

2. The Seventh-day Adventist lifestyle does contain privileges and prohibitions (dos and don'ts).

A. List the lifestyle prohibitions you feel in your own life.
B. List an equal number of lifestyle privileges (pleasant and desirable activities) that are encouraged for Seventh-day Adventists. See if you can find a scriptural reference that provides a rationale for each item on both of your lists.

3. Keeping the five principles of evaluation for lifestyle choices in mind, select two hours of "potentially beneficial" television viewing for this week. Videotape those hours, and then analyze the shows and the commercials for the following:

A. Positive humor
B. Philosophy of life
C. Spiritual encouragement
D. Men treated poorly
E. Values
F. Swear words
G. Affirming words
H. Proper conflict resolution
I. Violent acts
J. Rationalization of immoral behavior
K. Women treated poorly
L. Sexual implications

4. We often focus on jewelry as a sticky lifestyle issue, but there are many other activities and items that are not generally called "adornment" but that could be included here. We've given five to stimulate your thinking. List ten more.

1. Mag wheels
2. $45 silk ties
3. *Guess* jeans
4. 5,000-square-foot houses
5. Lexus automobiles

5. As you look at your list of items from 4, remember that many people become possessed by their possessions. A famous Christian hymn links simplicity with freedom: " 'Tis a gift to be simple, 'tis a gift to be free . . ." Jesus calls us to the *freedom of simplicity*, in which we have time and resources available for His kingdom work.

Simplicity does *not* mean living in confining poverty, but it does mean living with clear priorities.

Identify six ways you could *simplify your lifestyle* in order to free up *time* (three ways) and *resources* (three ways) to better serve Christ.

. . . .

 Focus Questions

1. How do we know which "standards" are biblically based and which are the result of our culture?
2. Is a gold crown jewelry?
3. What are the differences between watching a movie in a theater and watching it at home?
4. Why do all churches develop a list of lifestyle "dos and don'ts"?
5. Why does God give us freedom and then immediately tell us to serve Him and others? Doesn't that take away the freedom He has given us?
6. Is it possible for a person to be happy without having satisfying relationships with other people?

ELEGANCE

Love to God purifies and ennobles every taste and desire, intensifies every affection, and brightens every worthy pleasure (*Counsels to Teachers,* 53).

Dating: Love Within Limits

Lesson Scripture: Matthew 7:12

"Treat other people exactly as you would like to be treated by them—this is the essence of all true religion" (Matthew 7:12, Phillips).

"God's plan is to make you holy, and that entails first of all a clean cut with sexual immorality. Every one of you should learn to control his body, keeping it pure and treating it with respect, and never regarding it as an instrument for self-gratification, as do pagans with no knowledge of God. You cannot break this rule without in some way cheating your fellow men. . . . It is not for nothing that the Spirit God gives us is called the *Holy* Spirit" (1 Thessalonians 4:3-6a, 8b, Phillips).

"Will you go with me to the academy Fall Festival?" she asked. The student body's official "reverse weekend" marked the first significant dating event at school. Everybody knew that if things worked out, the guy would return the date for the Christmas banquet. The Valentine banquet could cement the relationship, and who knows, maybe the couple would be married the following summer.

Wait a minute. What ninth-grader really wants to be married before their tenth-grade year? Or who would admit it? Maybe they would just go together, and marriage could come much later, at a more opportune time. Anyway, if she didn't ask now, she knew another girl planned to ask him after the next class period.

That's why the request wasn't too original.

But he said, "Yes."

Could it be possible that he liked her? She had admired this "older man," a tenth-grader, for more than a week already. Perhaps this was just meant to be.

Then he asked, "Which one are you?"

Being a twin, Judy frequently had to clarify her identity. But surely Tony knew who she was. I mean, she had been watching him so many days; certainly he must have been checking her out too. Evidently guys are just a little slower than girls, especially twin girls.

"I'm Judy" provided all the information he needed.

Judy's sister, Julie, asked a ninth-grader, Tim, to go with her to the school party. "Since our names both begin with *J* and their names begin with *T*, maybe this will really be the start of something," the girls giggled.

The night of the Fall Festival provided quite a scenario for couples. Of course, the regular couples were together. But the new couples sparked the most notice. Some seemed natural together. Others obviously were mismatched, and it showed in their awkwardness.

Those who went stag acted like they were having fun, but you really wondered. And then there were several group dates, with an uneven number of males and females. They seemed to have fun, but they weren't experiencing the romance that couples have, or at least might have.

Come to think of it, some of the couples didn't seem to have any romantic spark. In fact, some seemed afraid of it. Others should have been afraid of it, but weren't. Maybe too much was at stake for one date.

Judy wondered if Tony would ask her to the Christmas banquet. If he didn't, everyone would know that he didn't like her enough to return her date. There was so much pressure. And what if she found somebody else? But Tony asked her before the next Mr. Wonderful did.

Would her sister, Julie, be paired with Tim for the rest of her life? Judy wondered if she would want Tim for a brother-in-law. Wait, this isn't a marriage thing. It's only dating. How is this dating stuff supposed to work? How did they do it in Bible times?

ARE YOU SURE THE BIBLE WANTS US TO DO THAT?

One of the great love stories found in the first book of the Bible relates the experience of Isaac and Rebekah. First of all, in those days, females were treated more like property than like humans. Rebekah's father and brothers were the ones to be convinced she should marry a relative whom none of them, including Rebekah, had ever seen. Few North American women would appreciate this type of arrangement in our culture today.

The dating experience of Isaac and Rebekah seems quite brief. Their first encounter resembles a chance occurrence as Isaac takes an evening walk and crosses paths with the returning servant and Rebekah. Before the engaged couple even meet, Rebekah covers her face with a veil. The servant relates the story of how he met Rebekah, his prayer and God's answer, and how the male relatives agreed for him to take her back to Isaac. Then "Isaac led Rebekah into his tent and made her his wife" (Genesis 24:67, Jerusalem Bible).

What ninth-grade male would want to be like Isaac and have a friend pick out a female whom he takes into his room on the first date and is then married for the rest of his life? And what ninth-grade female would want to be used in that way?

It wasn't much better for Isaac and Rebekah's son Jacob. Although he got to see the woman of his dreams, he had to wait and work for her seven years before he could finally marry her. Imagine finding the woman of your dreams and then waiting seven years before getting married. That shows some real restraint and patience!

The custom was to have a week-long wedding banquet. The first night the bride was taken to Jacob. How would you react if, after sleeping with your new wife, you woke up in the light of morning and discovered that she was not your betrothed, but her older sister? To make matters worse, this older sister was now your wife! And how do you suppose Rachel felt about this whole situation?

After the banquet, Jacob married Rachel also. Is it any wonder there were problems now that the two sisters were both married to Jacob, especially in light of the deception involved?

While some cultures continue to practice this, most people in North America don't, so it seems odd and even reprehensible to be tied to such a system today. We feel more accustomed to dating prior to marriage and getting married at a later age. While this permits independently minded people to select their own mates at their own time, our more recent history of unhappy marriages doesn't indicate that we've done a very good job with this system.

THERE MUST BE AN EXPLANATION

The Bible says virtually nothing about dating. That's logical, since people had arranged marriages in that culture, and such unions were made early in the teen years, about the age of ninth-graders. ⚊

 # Memory Focus

"Treat other people exactly as you would like to be treated by them—this is the essence of all true religion" (Matthew 7:12, Phillips).

. . . .

 # Into the Bible

Before we toss out the Bible as an out-of-date or out-of-place word from God, remember that the principles of the Bible are timeless and cross-cultural. That means the Bible can show us God's ideal for our dating situation, provided we identify the principles and apply them to our cultural practice called dating. So let's get into the Bible.

1. List biblical principles for dating relationships based on the passages below.
   A. Matthew 22:36-40
   B. John 15:12, 13
   C. Matthew 7:12
   D. 1 Thessalonians 4:3-10
   E. Ephesians 5:21-29, 32

2. Read all sixty-seven verses of Genesis 24. List at least four spiritual principles that apply to dating relationships today.

3. Write a one- to two-sentence paraphrase for each of the following texts about romantic relationships with people outside of one's faith.
   A. Deuteronomy 7:1, 3, 4, 6
   B. 1 Kings 11:1-4
   C. Nehemiah 13:23-27
   D. 2 Corinthians 6:14-18

4. Listed below are three different dating situations. Read the
   texts, and write the issues or principles that apply to that
   situation:
   A. Dating outside the Christian faith:
      (1) Romans 12:2
      (2) Ephesians 5:1-5
      (3) 1 Kings 11:1-4
   B. Dating outside the Seventh-day Adventist Church:
      (1) Genesis 24:1-4
      (2) Ruth 1:16
   C. Dating within the Seventh-day Adventist Church:
      (1) 2 Corinthians 6:14
      (2) 2 Timothy 2:22
      (3) 1 Corinthians 5:9-11

. . . .

 Projects

1. Divide the class into two groups, the males in one group and
   the females in another group. Each group needs to come to a
   consensus on the following two areas:

   A. A prioritized list of ten things they look for in the opposite
      sex.
   B. A prioritized list of ten things they think the other group
      would look for in them.

   When the lists have been developed, the groups should report
   the results to the class. How similar are they? The group should
   discuss similarities in the two lists and how they show a foundation of biblical principles.
2. Love and lust are exact opposites. The initial feelings may seem
   similar, but the attitudes, actions, and outcomes are different.
   On the worksheet your teacher supplies, look over the list of
   phrases, and mark with an *O* each phrase that describes lust.
   Mark with an *X* each phrase that describes love.

3. Form small groups, and develop lists of ideas for the following two topics. Once the lists have been completed, share the ideas and/or suggestions with the class.

   A. Realistic and effective ways to deal with the issue of pre-marital sex.
   B. The options and consequences when it comes to teen pregnancy.

· ·

 Focus Questions

1. What is the purpose of dating?
2. Describe the difference between a friendship and a romance.
3. What are some practical guidelines for wholesome dating?
4. How does a person's self-image affect dating experiences?
5. Some people say that sex is an expression of love. Do you agree or disagree? Why?
6. Why is the relationship between Christ and His people often likened to lovers and marriage in both the Old and New Testaments?

GENTLENESS

Deal kindly with others. There are often tears in the heart that never reach the eye *(Quips and Quotes)*.

Wanted: Family Ties

Lesson Scripture: Exodus 20:12, NIV

Eloping provides a way to escape from all that's involved in a wedding ceremony. Although children often play at getting married, some adults prefer to bypass the wedding ceremony.

Wedding gown, bridal attendant dresses, tuxedos for the guys, flowers, the right church, music, photographer, videographer, the minister, announcements, relatives, the reception, the cost—it's enough to intimidate anyone.

But whether you choose to elope or to have a wedding ceremony, the product of both is the same—a family. Some choose not to marry so that they won't have the responsibilities of a family. Yet even the unmarried are part of a family based on their origin, other relatives, adoptive people, and sometimes friends who function as family.

Families provide one way of describing who we are. A family name provides a point of reference and carries a certain reputation with it. The custom in North America is for a female to take her spouse's last name when she marries. A few prefer to not lose their maiden name and have a joint married name. Even so, one's family of origin can still influence a person, no matter how much one tries to deny or transcend it.

And what affects other members of your family will affect you. After all, they're part of your family. No wonder books abound regarding families— how to have a happy one, how to break the unfortunate cycles

241

that seem to continue from generation to generation, starting a new family, having or not having children, parenting, rekindling love, birth order, and how to get along with your parents.

The Bible contains a wide assortment of family experiences. Adam and Eve's family contains quite an array. A wife leads a husband astray. Their sons quarrel to the point of murder. Yet the Saviour of the world is still promised through their descendants.

Noah's family demonstrated solidarity by staying together and entering the ark, even though it had never rained and they were ridiculed for their decision. But even their family couldn't keep it together, as evidenced by the rebellion that led to the Tower of Babel and the ensuing language confusion and dispersion of the many relatives.

Eventually God chose to reveal Himself to and through the family of Abram (who later was named Abraham by God). It began with a call by God and trust by Abram to rely totally on one God rather than to rely on many gods, as everyone else seemed to do.

In responding to God's call, Abram still had family considerations that affected what he did. First of all, out of respect for his father, he traveled only as far as his father's health would allow and even took a long stay in Haran. Abram's brother, Nahor, possibly was with the group or else moved to Haran later. It was from Nahor's family line that a wife was sought for Isaac. Other relatives must have stayed in the secure comforts of Ur, with the exception of Abram's adventurous nephew, Lot, who followed him to Haran and later to Canaan.

Family ties can hold when other considerations falter. And family ties get more entwined when families become intermarried, as Abram's family eventually became. Being selected as God's special people resulted in certain directives from the Lord, but a number of local customs were acceptable, appropriate, and adopted by Abram's family.

When Adam and Eve were made for each other, there weren't other options available. They couldn't date anyone else. As the population increased, securing a mate offered a decision-making opportunity. Evidently the human race hadn't degenerated to the point of causing abnormal children from marrying and having children within one's own bloodline.

The same was true in the time of Abram. Knowing the tremendous influence a spouse has on a person, God counseled His people to marry within their religious culture, maintaining their commitment to one God rather than the many gods of other cultures. That's why Abraham sent his trusted servant, Eliezer, to secure a wife for Isaac, the son of promise, from his relatives who had traveled as far as Haran. And that's why Isaac and Rebekah later sent Jacob to Haran.

That was thousands of years ago. Things change. At least some things change. But others remain the same. Consider the similarities and differences in weddings and marriages in Abram's day and in ours.

Abram lived in a male-dominated society. A male, the father of the groom, initiated the engagement. The family of the bride, especially the potential bride's father and brothers, had to be considered. Even though males seemed to take the lead in the arrangements, females weren't necessarily left out of the discussion.

God's people were to marry within their own community of faith. Otherwise, there would be a social and cultural breakdown that could threaten the faith and religion of God's people.

Getting married proved to be more than just a social arrangement. Financial ramifications needed to be considered. The father of the bride received a fee or marriage present from the groom's family. This should not be misunderstood as purchasing the bride like a piece of property. It demonstrated that the new man of the house was capable of providing for his new wife. It also served as an acknowledgment that the bride was a gift of great worth.

If a marriage present was not possible, a man could work for the father of the bride, as Jacob did. Special or heroic acts could accomplish the same thing.

Continuing the family was one of the major purposes of marriage. In agrarian (farming) societies, children functioned as workers in the family business. The more workers there were, the greater the likelihood that a family would be prosperous. That's why a large number of children were considered a blessing and why females so

often seemed to serve as continuous baby makers.

This also explains part of the reason for polygamy—to enlarge one's family for the benefit of all. It also shows the purpose of the levirate law in which a widow was to marry the brother of her deceased husband if she had no sons yet. This preserved the family name and property and prevented marriage to outsiders. There's no doubt that being a family involved a number of ties, regardless of the circumstances.

The wedding ceremony in Bible times certainly seemed far from an elopement. Through betrothal, a promise for the marriage was set. The marriage present was given to the bride's father, but there was still some time before the engaged couple actually were married and lived together.

The bride had special attire for the wedding. Both the bride and groom had attendants. The wedding feast could last for a week or longer. The marriage ceremony did not conclude until the bride and groom went into a special tent or room prepared as a wedding chamber for them. It was here that they first had intercourse, thereby consummating the marriage.

In North America, some customs are different, while others are very similar to those of Bible times. In the Middle East and the Far East, most of these customs continue to this day. A wedding and marriage form a critical union for the individuals, for the families, and for the society as a whole. The ties that result make up a great deal of what we consider to be "family."

What is *your* family like today? Less than one hundred years ago, most families in North America were very large. Not only were there many children in a family, but the family stayed together through the generations, with aunts and uncles and cousins all living together. Some referred to this as the extended family, since the family extended to so many people.

As an increasing number of people moved to cities, large families turned out to be a financial liability rather than a financial asset. Parents decided to have fewer children, and there were not as many extended families. Eventually a new term came into vogue—the nuclear family, which described the family of four, Mom and Dad, plus two children, usually a boy and girl.

In the past several decades, divorce has become so common in North America, and in the Adventist Church, that the nuclear family seems more like an exception than the norm. Someone in your own family, or your extended family, quite likely has experienced divorce. Most can testify to the hardships that result from a broken family. Except in cases of abuse, rarely will someone say that their life after a divorce is as good as it was before. For the most part, families continue to be a source of stability and joy, while broken families are often a source of insecurity and pain.

Perhaps that's why some people have tried living together without getting married. Their fear of becoming another divorce statistic prevents them from making a commitment to another person through marriage. They figure that the pain of divorce won't touch them. But neither will the joy and security of marriage. They will discover that living together actually creates tremendous insecurity because of the lack of commitment. Your partner can give up on you at any time.

Adventuresome teens and those in their twenties who seem to "know it all" may be on the move to check out as many people as possible or to find that perfect one for them, but the yearnings for security and intimacy only seem to increase as the years go by. And while many families are poor models of this ideal, others give glimpses that stir hope that possibly you, too, could be part of a family that would provide deep ties. Instead of simply hoping for that to be a reality for you, consider what the Bible has to say. You'll be surprised at some of the things you'll find. Although some things are different today, you'll be amazed to discover how many things apply to your contemporary situation. ⨯

💿 Memory Focus

"Honor your father and mother. This is the first of God's Ten Commandments that ends with a promise. And this is the promise: that if you honor your father and mother, yours will be a long life, full of blessing" (Ephesians 6:2, 3, TLB).

 Into the Bible

1. At the beginning of this world and shortly after the Flood, people had no choice but to marry relatives. Apparently the human race had not degenerated enough that this would cause abnormal children to be born. Use the worksheet your teacher will supply and the texts below to chart the family tree of Terah. Note the marriages within the family and what family relationship existed prior to marriage.

   A. Genesis 11:27-32
   B. Genesis 19:30-38
   C. Genesis 20:11-13
   D. Genesis 24:15
   E. Genesis 25:19-21, 24-26
   F. Genesis 29:16, 26-28

2. When it came time for Isaac to be married, Abraham sent his trusted servant, Eliezer, back to his own country to find a wife for his son from among his own relatives. Eliezer did not hesitate to pray under such circumstances. Read this first recorded prayer in the Bible in Genesis 24:12-14. Although it is brief, answer the following:

   A. To whom is Eliezer praying, and what is the significance of this?
   B. What generally did he ask for?
   C. What specifically did he ask for?
   D. What were the results? (See verses 15-19, 50, 51.)

3. List seven principles from the Bible texts below that provide guidance for relationships between parents and children:

   A. Exodus 20:12
   B. Deuteronomy 6:5-9
   C. Joshua 4:4-7
   D. Proverbs 6:20
   E. Ephesians 6:1-3
   F. Ephesians 6:4
   G. Colossians 3:21

4. In the following biblical examples, identify the attitudes and actions that lessened the sanctity of marriage and undermined family togetherness:

   A. Genesis 16:1-6; 21:1-3
   B. Genesis 27:5-10, 35
   C. 2 Samuel 13:7-21, 28, 29
   D. 1 Corinthians 5:1-5

. . . .

 Projects

1. Contact at least four separate families, and ask two family members separately what they would consider to be their top four family values.

Compare the responses. Then list your top four family values. Share the results of your survey and your own values with the class.

2. Divide into small groups that will function as family units. Each group should have a father and/or a mother, a ninth-grader, and a twenty-year-old brother or sister living at home. Other members of the group can have other identities to complete the family, such as a ten-year-old sibling, a grandparent, another teen, etc. Discuss the following issues as a family, and identify the principles your family will follow.

    A. Should there be a curfew? If so, when is it?
    B. Who pays for clothes? Academy tuition?
    C. What activities will the family do together?
    D. Where will the family go on vacation, and who will decide?
    E. What role will religion play in your family?
    F. At what age(s) will children help determine the rules?

3. Skim through current newspapers and magazines, and cut out articles depicting actions and/or attitudes that promote the sanctity of marriage and family togetherness. Share the articles with the class.

4. Draw your family tree, representing at least four generations. Then respond to the following:

    A. How large is your family?
    B. How close do the generations live to each other?
    C. How often do they see each other?
    D. Which relatives do you feel the closest to, and why?

 # Focus Questions

1. How should a family operate: as a democracy, dictatorship, do your own thing, etc.?
2. How much voice do you have in your family? How much do you think you should have?
3. What can *you* do to combat the forces that undermine marriage and family togetherness?
4. How much time does your family spend together during a typical week? Would you prefer your family to spend more time together or less time together? Why?
5. Which principles from the Bible apply to your situation and what you are likely to face in the future? Explain. (See Into the Bible 3 and 4.)

SAFETY

The freedom God provides has built-in limits for our good—laws that protect us from evil and safeguard our happiness *(Gordon Kainer)*.

lesson 27

That's the Way Love Works

Lesson Scripture: Psalm 103:13, 14, NIV

As a father has compassion on his children, so the Lord has compassion on those who fear him; for he knows how we are formed, he remembers that we are dust" (Psalm 103:13, 14, NIV).

Kathy wasn't about to make the same mistake her parents had made. Since she knew firsthand what it was like to live through and with the effects of a dirty divorce, she determined to experiment before making a lifetime commitment to a marriage partner. Divorce simply was too painful to go through again, and there wouldn't be any children to suffer because two adults couldn't get along.

Once she realized that Mr. Wonderful was a myth, she found Mr. Acceptable, and they got an apartment together. It was good to get out of the house and be on her own. Tom was making fairly good money and going to night school. Kathy went to the community college and worked part time in retail. It took a lot of money to live on their own, especially to get started, but sharing the expenses made it more manageable.

That's one of the beauties of living together, Kathy thought. *It costs half as much as living by yourself.* When she noticed that Tom seemed to have more money available than she had, he pointed out that he worked longer hours at a job that paid more than Kathy's. Since they

249

split the living costs in half, he was left with more extra money than Kathy.

Although Tom gave Kathy a $20 bill every once in a while, it seemed like she was getting an allowance from her daddy, and $20 didn't buy much.

When they first started having sex, Kathy felt a little guilty. While she had been brought up believing that sex outside of marriage was wrong, her parents weren't exactly good examples, and if she was going to try this living-together arrangement, sex was part of the package. Sometimes it was lots of fun. Admittedly, at other times she felt as if she was being used.

After six months, things seemed to be in a routine. Living together wasn't all that exciting. Tom seemed to take Kathy for granted. She really felt hurt when she found out he was seeing somebody else. But Tom pointed out that she was free to do the same. They weren't married, just living together.

So Kathy found somebody else to go out with her. Maybe this would make Tom jealous and he would take a greater interest in her. Ken was a nice-enough guy. When they became

physically involved, it threw Kathy for a loop. She remembered that sex was for marriage. But she already had given up that life commandment. Sex had become what you share with the person you live with. But the person she lived with was dating somebody else. In fact, she liked Ken more than Tom right now.

Before Kathy knew it, she and Ken had made love. Afterward, Ken seemed satisfied, but Kathy felt empty. If that was making love, then love is a hollow feeling. Kathy wondered if she should move in with Ken, but his apartment was worse than the one she was in already.

Eventually, Tom's relationship with the other woman ended. It was sort of like Tom and Kathy got together again while they were living together. They resumed sexual relations, except this time Tom transmitted herpes to Kathy.

She was furious! If he hadn't gone out on her, he never would have gotten that sexually transmitted disease. Now he had passed it on to her. Was that love? She felt so dirty, so infected, so used and abused.

Tom told her she could leave if she wanted. She did want to, but where would she go? She didn't make enough money to live on her own. Should she try to move in with Ken? Would he even want her now that she was infected? Maybe she shouldn't tell him. He could just be surprised, like she had been when she contracted herpes. No, he probably wouldn't like it any more than she did. At least it wasn't AIDS.

Maybe she should move back home. But which home? Which parent? She had really burned the bridges with her mother. It didn't seem likely that she would get much of a welcome. Her father had married a woman Kathy couldn't stand. And he traveled a lot, so he wasn't home much. That meant Kathy would be living with his wife.

Complications increased when Kathy found out she was pregnant. She wasn't even certain who the father was. Abortion wasn't an option for her. Having a child would further strain her financial situation and limit her ability to date, much less find a man who would want her and her child.

Kathy's life seemed as though it was racing downhill. She didn't know if it would be best to bail out now or wait for

the impact at the bottom. Then she remembered the story of the prodigal son. The details weren't exactly the same for her, but she remembered that the father had been waiting and watching each day for the child to return home. Her father

wasn't doing that, but she also remembered the father in the story represented God, who is ready to accept us just as we are and is eager to wrap His loving arms around us and announce that we are His children.

Kathy prayed for the first time in quite a while. She sensed the peace of acceptance by God even though it didn't resolve her living situation. She went to a nearby Seventh-day Adventist church. Although there weren't many people her age, there were a few. Maybe it was time to expand her friendships beyond just her peers.

She met Tonya, who was a few years older. What an incredible contrast! Tonya had basically followed all those rules Kathy knew were right. Her parents hadn't been perfect either. But Tonya didn't use that as an excuse to dump what she knew was right. She wasn't living with a guy or being used by another guy. She didn't have a sexually transmitted disease, nor was she pregnant.

Only a few years had elapsed since academy graduation, and already the results of choices made seemed to make the correct choice obvious. Kathy clung to the assurance of God's forgiveness of her mistakes. But she wished she had followed more of the rules that would have prevented so many of her current problems. Now she knew what people had meant when they said that God's rules were simply instructions for having a better life.

Kathy convinced Tonya that the two of them should share their contrasting testimonies in the youth room at church so the young people would be encouraged to stay with God's instruction instead of messing around until they wanted God's forgiveness. What surprised Kathy most was that the youth seemed to be more interested in her lifestyle than Tonya's. Would it take as much heartache for them as it had for Kathy to take God at His word?

Whose experience appeals to you—Kathy's or Tonya's? Kathy's life seemed to be filled with adventure. She felt a certain liberty and maturity as she disregarded rules she had heard since childhood. When nobody was there to impose them on her, she tossed them aside. They certainly had been part of her values. And when the negative consequences she'd always heard about didn't happen to her right away, she figured they were just scare tactics used to intimidate teens. Living in a fantasy world, she figured, "It won't happen to me."

Although reality demolished Kathy's fantasy, God still had good news for her, which may be good news for you too.

Because of God's incredible love, He doesn't give up on us, and He provides the best for us even when we mess up. If you doubt that, consider the way He has treated people through the ages who messed up BIG time—people like Abraham, Jacob, Samson, King David, and the children of Israel! God's love gives a sense of acceptance when we don't think anyone, especially God, accepts us. And God's forgiveness provides peace of mind and an end to the gnawing feelings of guilt that are a natural result of blowing it.

In addition to acceptance and forgiveness, there's more good news about God's love. God's love goes beyond an ambulance service at the bottom of a cliff when you crash. God also puts up a fence at the top of the cliff to prevent you from the fall. You don't have to fall or even jump off the cliff.

The Bible not only shows how God forgave and accepted people, but His love also shows ways to *really* live. Some people say, "Get a life." That's what God has in mind for you. That kind of life pleases God, and it certainly will please you.

You can be sure God's love for you is constant. But He gives you the choice of living His way in the first place and enjoying the benefits of godly living or doing it your own way and suffering the consequences. Some say that's not much of a choice. Others say it's an easy choice.

One thing is certain. Being loved regardless of our choices is something we aren't apt to experience anywhere else in this world. But then, isn't that what you would expect from God? ⟑

 **Memory Focus**

"As a father has compassion on his children, so the Lord has compassion on those who fear him" (Psalm 103:13, NIV).

. . . .

 Into the Bible

1. Using the worksheet provided by your teacher, write what you believe the Bible says regarding divorce and remarriage in selected passages.
2. Use the worksheet provided by your teacher to show how God revealed His character of love, compassion, and forgiveness to Adam and Eve.
3. Use the worksheet provided by your teacher to show how God's character of love, compassion, and forgiveness was also demonstrated in the family of Abram (Abraham).
4. God's revelation of His character didn't end with Abraham. Read the following passages, and describe examples of God's love, compassion, and forgiveness as demonstrated to Jacob.

   A. Genesis 28:10-17
   B. Genesis 32:9-12, 30; 33:4

5. Read Deuteronomy 4:5-14; Hebrews 12:4-13; and Ephesians 6:4; then explain:

   A. The role of authority as it relates to God.
   B. The role of authority as it relates to parents.

6. Use the worksheet provided by your teacher to examine examples from the Bible of positive or negative methods used by parents for dealing with their children.

 **Projects**

1. Identify what you think Jennifer's parents and Ryan's parents did right and what they did wrong in the following situations. What are some realistic alternatives they could have used? Use the worksheet provided by your teacher.

    A. Jennifer was in trouble for being more than an hour late for curfew and then lying about having car trouble. Her parents were so angry that they grounded her for a month. That meant no Valentine's banquet for Jennifer. She was so disappointed with their choice of discipline that she rudely talked back to her parents and then added several expletives to show she was angry too. Her mother immediately slapped Jennifer's face. "I'll not have you talk like that to me," her mother retorted. "And, furthermore, you've not kept up with your assigned household chores. You'll have your chores and the chores of your brother to do for the next month." Jennifer threatened to run away, but instead, she ran to her room and locked the door. She decided she wouldn't ever speak to her parents again.

    B. Ryan thought his parents were going to get him for cheating at school, but the school principal had told his parents about something else. The vandalism at the academy from breaking in and shooting off the fire extinguisher in the library would be costly. One of the guys in the group already had admitted that all of them were drunk when they did it. Now his parents had figured out that he had stolen money from their wallets to get the booze. "We thought you received enough allowance so you wouldn't have to steal, especially from your own parents," they said. "We don't know if we should take away your keys to your BMW or what. You know how we feel about drinking and driving. We know you're not in a situation to pay for the costs to clean up the library. We just want you to know that we're really disappointed in what you did. Do you realize

what other people are going to think about our family now?" Ryan apologized profusely for embarrassing his parents and offered to spend part of next Sunday weeding one of the flower beds in the backyard as punishment for his mistake. His parents said that wasn't necessary, as long as he didn't pull a stunt like that again.

2. How is parenting today different from your parents' generation? How is it the same? Write down your own ideas. Then ask another teen, the parent of a teen, and the grandparent of a teen. Compare the responses. Use the worksheet your teacher provides.

3. Research indicates that most Christian parents face five troubling major issues in their families. Any of them may be present at different times, or some may be present at the same time. Fill out the worksheet "Five Cries of Parents," available from your teacher.

4. Analyze the benefits of sexual purity before marriage as well as during marriage. What are the physical, social, emotional, and spiritual benefits of being sexually pure? Use the worksheet "Sexual Purity," provided by the teacher.

5. Identify four prevalent values promoted or portrayed in the media (TV, movies, magazines).

6. Write a statement that expresses your personal opinion on two of the following issues. Then identify an outside source (such as specific things you've read, seen, or heard from people you know; advertising in the media; music; etc.) that supports your opinion or perhaps helped shape it in the first place.

   A. How high a priority should be placed on the pursuit of material affluence.
   B. What you think of the guidance you get from church.
   C. What reasons you would offer for the importance of a close family.
   D. What you think of people who choose to dedicate their lives to service, such as missionaries, Peace Corps volunteers, etc.
   E. Whether you will dedicate your life to service. What you hope to receive for this.

 **Focus Questions**

1. Is it all right, from God's perspective, for divorced people to get remarried if there hasn't been adultery?
2. What are the issues in living together before marriage?
3. In what ways do your parents have authority over you? How does that compare with God's authority over you?
4. What is the Seventh-day Adventist Church's official position on abortion? Do you agree or disagree?
5. What is your school doing regarding AIDS? What do you think your school should do?
6. People sometimes argue about whether or not music affects people. What evidence can you give that it does or doesn't affect people? How does it affect you?

INDECISION

No person chooses evil because it is evil; he only mistakes it for happiness, the good he seeks *(Mary Shelley)*.

An Adventist Advantage

Lesson Scripture: 1 Peter 2:9, NIV

Can you imagine what school was like thousands of years ago? What classes do you think you might have taken back then if you had lived in one of the most advanced nations of that time? In what ways do you suppose school was different from today?

To be more precise, let's take a look at a classroom scene as it might have been 3,500 years ago. It's a university setting (or whatever schools like that were called back then), and the class is made up largely of older students—priests, government officials, and doctors, and even some members of the royal family are present.

As we venture inside the classroom, we see a distinguished-looking gentleman talking about modern medicine and the latest techniques in health care. As we listen, he pauses for a moment to ask his students a question. "What would you do for a patient who has a disease that results in the loss of hair?"

After a few moments of silence, a handsome young man stands up, bows to the professor, and, speaking with a slight accent, he says, "Sir, to prevent the loss of hair, I would apply a mixture of six fats taken from a horse, a crocodile, a hippopotamus, a cat, a snake, and a wild goat. If that doesn't take care of the problem, I would anoint the person's head with honey mixed with the crushed tooth of a donkey!"

All heads now turn back toward the professor as he

responds. "An excellent answer, young man. And since we're on the topic of hair," the professor continues, "can you tell the class how you would keep a person's hair from turning gray?"

Without hesitation, the student replies, "Sir, I would soak the hair with the blood of a black calf that has been boiled in olive oil or apply the fat of a rattlesnake."

Sounds too weird and farfetched to be true, you say? How could anyone in his or her right mind ever use gross stuff like that? Well, that wasn't a problem only in the distant past. Keep in mind that people have used all kinds of mysterious potions and magical tonics right up to the present time.

But let's get back to that scholarly young man in the classroom. Acts 7:22 states, "Moses was educated in all the wisdom of the Egyptians and was powerful in speech and action" (NIV). And what about those unusual prescriptions he was expounding to the class? They were actual medical prescriptions taken from a famous medical journal entitled *Papyrus Ebers*, written about the year 1552 B.C.[1]

Other so-called remedies in this ancient medical scroll for ordinary wounds or open sores include hot worms' blood, decayed flesh, moisture from pigs' ears, as well as waste products from cats, dogs, and even flies. No wonder it's been said that humans die as much from their cures as from their diseases.

Of course, not all of their ideas regarding diet and healthful living were off the mark. Egyptians inscribed on the walls of the pyramids the common foods eaten by the builder, including a large assortment of leeks, onions, and garlic. (Can you imagine the aroma that must have surrounded those ancient building sites?) Leeks were used in thirty-two medical compounds. Because onions and garlic had proven themselves to be definite contributors to hale and healthy bodies, they were considered foods given by the gods and were found in twenty-six medical prescriptions.

After the Israelites left Egypt during the Exodus, the Bible records that they wanted to continue eating the food of the

[1]S. I. McMillan, M.D., *None of These Diseases* (Grand Rapids, Mich.: Fleming H. Revell Company, 1963).

Egyptians that they had come to like so well. Not only did they enjoy stimulating tastes and exotic flavors; they probably felt that this was the best food for them at the time.

But in His wisdom, God provided His people with something vastly superior—the most nourishing food, remedies that truly healed, as well as comprehensive instructions for a truly healthy lifestyle. Egypt had a highly developed medical practice. Its doctors performed surgery, used antiseptics, and employed drugs for curing a wide variety of diseases. But the health laws that Moses received from God did not focus on *prescriptions*, but rather on *prevention*. Divine guidelines were given regarding personal cleanliness and hygiene; camp sanitation; the need for proper food, attire, rest, and exercise; and the importance of moral purity.

God desired the very best for Israel. He promised them that if they followed through with His directions, they would not suffer from any of the diseases that were so common among the Egyptians. And to start off with, God replaced the "junk food" of Egypt with daily portions of the "bread from heaven," known to us as manna.

God's ultimate objective was to lead them step by step to unparalleled prosperity. Through an abiding relationship with Him, they were to be His holy people, "blessed more than any other people." In practical skills and craftsmanship; in intellect and sound judgment; and in physical, mental, and spiritual attainments, they were to excel and be "high above all the nations." The Israelites were God's chosen representatives among the nations of the earth. And it was His plan that all these nations would come to recognize the tremendous advantages of those who place their trust in God and practice the principles of heaven.

As believers in Jesus, we stand as God's witnesses in today's world. Like Israel of old, it is our privilege to demonstrate in everyday life the spiritual and practical advantages of being a Christian. The most important lesson in Christian living that we must learn and pass on to others is that what God *provides* is always for our good, and whatever He *prohibits* is never for our good. Even for Christians, this may be hard, at times, to accept. Sometimes this

biblical truth is very quickly and vividly revealed; at other times it only becomes evident over an extended period of time. The Bible clearly illustrates this principle by its stories, its history, and its teachings. For the followers of God, therefore, the question whether *any* sin is ever a good thing should be a settled issue. Isn't it surprising how often we waver on this crucial point?

As the Jewish people sometimes did, the Christian church has often forsaken many of the guidelines and high ideals that are taught in the Bible. People seek happiness at the expense of holiness. Christ-centered living is gradually replaced by living from the world's point of view. In response, God sets into motion spiritual movements that will restore and revive essential truths that have been ignored and forgotten. The Seventh-day Adventist Church sees itself as involved in this very mission.

The Adventist way of life is designed to provide spiritual insight and practical guidance for Christians who live in the last days of earth's history. We believe Jesus Christ, our only Saviour from sin, offers "abun-dant life" to all who believe in Him and obey His Word (John 10:10). In other words, sharing the good news leads to living the good life.

An important premise of Christianity is that it is always an advantage to be on God's side, to obey His will in His way. The advantage is not from us. It is bestowed by God. But keep in mind that God does not play favorites. What is described in this lesson as the "Adventist advantage" refers to spiritual benefits that are available to all. Any person or church can share in this advantage if they are willing to put biblical Christianity into practice. The Bible's invitation to "taste and see that the Lord is good" is graciously extended to all.

On the other hand, apart from the sustaining power and presence of God, the advantage He offers may seem a burden rather than a blessing. When experienced without love and trust in God, the Christian life can easily be viewed as restricting rather than enriching our lives, subtracting rather than adding to our happiness. Could this explain why there are professing Christians who feel that the Christian life is not an advantage at all? They think they are missing out on exciting things non-Christians are free to enjoy. How can anything be considered an advantage, they say, if it keeps you from enjoying all the good stuff that the world has to offer?

Human beings are basically self-centered. Our most common impulse is to cater to our own desires. But to put self as the center is death, so God offers each of us a new life through His Son. He enables us to experience living at its very best. Best, that is, from God's viewpoint. Our view is like looking at life through a knothole. It's narrow and short-sighted and focuses on what we can see right now. From such a perspective, we live for the "here and now" and disregard the warning labels and the price tags that accompany every choice we make.

In contrast to our limited peek at life, God's view encompasses all there is to see and know. Nothing is hidden from Him. He is intensely concerned with what is happening in our lives right now, but in His wisdom, He considers our entire life span and makes provision for eternity as well.

Imagine that when you were about a year old, someone offered you one hundred shiny new pennies in one hand and a $100,000 check in the other. Your baby instincts would have kicked into gear, and you would have quickly grabbed the shiny stuff. In fact, you might have become upset or even cried if you didn't get the pennies. But suppose someone told you now that you chose one dollar rather than $100,000. Your reaction would be predictable. In dismay you would blurt out, "Why didn't someone who understood help me make the right choice?"

God does help. He is the source of all true wisdom, the answer to all of life's problems, the fountain of all real love and happiness. He will walk by your side every day of your life. Walking with God is life's greatest advantage. ⚹

Memory Focus

"You are a chosen generation, a royal priesthood, a holy nation, His own special people, that you may proclaim the praises of Him who called you out of darkness into His marvelous light" (1 Peter 2:9, NKJV).

. . . .

 # Into the Bible

1. The narrative at the beginning of this lesson introduces the following key thoughts:

   • It is God Himself who gives us the wisdom to know how to live life at its best.
   • The natural human tendency is to reject God's authority and to turn away from the Christian way of life.
   • It is only the true Christian who enjoys and appreciates divine guidance.
   • There are positive results (advantages) that accompany obedience to God.
   • It is our privilege to demonstrate to the world the advantages of being a Christian.

   In this activity, you will study the Bible to see what it says regarding the important issues listed below. Read the following texts, and write a brief summary of each.

   A. What are the different ways God imparts His knowledge to us regarding the Christian life? What do we learn from these sources?

      (1) Romans 3:20; 7:7
      (2) Psalm 119:105; 2 Timothy 3:16, 17
      (3) John 16:13

   B. Apart from a relationship with Jesus, what is our natural response to God and spiritual things?

(1) Ephesians 2:3
(2) Romans 8:7
(3) Galatians 5:17

C. What inner changes of attitude will be found in the person who has accepted Jesus as his/her personal Saviour?

(1) John 15:10
(2) Galatians 5:24
(3) 2 Timothy 1:7

D. Though Christians are not saved because they obey God, saved people desire to obey God in response to the salvation they have freely received. What are some of the blessings of such obedience?

(1) Psalm 119:98, 99   (4) Proverbs 3:1, 2
(2) Psalm 119:165   (5) Deuteronomy 28:1
(3) Proverbs 7:1-5

E. What does the Bible say regarding the privileges and responsibilities of living the Christian life?

(1) 1 Peter 2:9   (2) 2 Corinthians 5:17-20

2. The Bible describes human beings as a special creation, made "in the image of God" (Genesis 1:27, NIV). Each person is a threefold union of body, soul, and spirit (1 Thessalonians 5:23) or heart, soul, and mind (Matthew 22:37). These function as a unit and reveal the intimate relationship between a person's physical, mental, and spiritual faculties.

Read the following texts, and explain how each describes the close ties between the physical, mental, and spiritual powers and how they affect one another.

A. Exodus 15:26   D. 1 Corinthians 6:19, 20
B. Psalm 103:1-3   E. 1 Corinthians 10:31
C. Proverbs 17:22   F. 3 John 1:2

3. In His Word, God has given us specific instructions and general guidelines on how we can prevent illness and promote physical, mental, and spiritual health. Read the following texts, and identify God's instructions. In addition, you may wish to in-

clude questions regarding the texts, which could be discussed during class time.

A. Leviticus 10:8, 9

B. Psalm 37:1, 7, 8

C. Proverbs 6:32

D. Luke 21:34

E. Romans 12:14, 19-21

F. Philippians 4:8

G. 1 Peter 5:6, 7

Projects

1. TEN-DAY PHYSICAL-FITNESS PROGRAM. Participate in a ten-day biblically based physical-fitness program, such as Daniel and his companions requested while captives in Babylon (Daniel 1:8-21).

   A. Read the first chapter of Daniel in two or three versions to gain a clear overview of the spiritual principles, health guidelines, and immediate benefits of Daniel's choice.

   B. As you participate in this project, keep an accurate daily record on the form provided by your teacher, and turn it in with your final report.

   C. Write a short summary describing the personal benefits you experienced (if any). Were there any negative effects? What seemed to help you the most? What was the most difficult part for you? Why?

   D. What are your personal reactions to such a fitness program? What do you think you might continue to do that you have not done in the past?

2. Interview a minimum of four people: a senior citizen (fifty-five or older), a parent, a classmate or friend, and one other person of your choice.

   The interview question is: What are the advantages and/or disadvantages of being raised a Seventh-day Adventist?

   After the interviews, compile your findings. In addition, report your reactions or conclusions to the interviews, as well as your own convictions on the question. Share the findings with the class.

3. Although Seventh-day Adventists have much in common with other Christians, there are some things we believe or practice that are unique to Seventh-day Adventists.

    A. Compile a list of beliefs, practices, or standards that are unique to the Seventh-day Adventist Church (that is, in comparison with other established churches).

    B. Explain the negative or positive effects that one or more of these have on a teenager's life.

 Focus Questions

1. What advantages have you found in the Seventh-day Adventist lifestyle?
2. Biblical health laws emphasize prevention rather than prescription. How do Seventh-day Adventists practice that principle today?
3. Which of God's prohibitions are most puzzling to you?
4. What does the following statement mean: "Every choice we make has a price tag"?
5. What keeps people from asking God's counsel or that His will be done when making important or minor decisions?
6. What would you say is a significant contribution the Seventh-day Adventist Church has made to the world? To other Christians?
7. Do you think that the Seventh-day Adventist Church prohibits certain things that are not prohibited in the Bible? What things?
8. How can the Seventh-day Adventist lifestyle enable us to better help people in the last days?

FORGIVENESS

We are most like beasts when we kill; most like men when we judge;
most like God when we forgive *(The Daily Walk)*.

lesson 29

The Family Says It All

Lesson Scripture: Genesis 37

I hate you!"

The words hung in the air like smoke from a bad cigar. Cyndy clapped her hand over her mouth as if she had tried to keep them in, but failed. Her dad just stood there with his mouth hanging open. Suddenly, Cyndy broke and ran up the stairs to her room.

Mr. Sanderson collapsed onto the couch. *What have I done?* he thought to himself. *What kind of father am I when my own daughter hates me?* He shuddered as he thought back to his own shouted words.

"No! I don't care what you want. You can't, and that's final!"

Cyndy's door slammed behind her as she stumbled onto her bed, eyes filled with tears. *Did I really say that?* she thought. *Did I really tell my own father that I hated him?* She banged her head against the mattress. *He just makes me so mad! Why can't he treat me like he does Angela? Just because she's two years older doesn't mean that I'm a child.*

Mr. Sanderson seemed unable to move from the couch. *Of course I care what she wants,* he said to himself. *She knows that, doesn't she? I wish I could let her do everything she wants, but she's just not old enough to deal with some situations. How can I make her understand? Without yelling at her.*

Cyndy's eyes began to dry. *I just want to be treated like a fifteen-year-old,* she thought. *I just want to be able to make some of my own decisions. I'm just as mature and responsible as Angela anyway. Didn't they have to ground her last*

month for coming in late? I'd never do that.

Mr. Sanderson stirred and opened his eyes. *Maybe I should allow her more freedom to do what she wants. I do want her to be able to make decisions, to develop responsibility. But I also want to protect her! She just doesn't realize how quick and easy it would be to get pulled into a mistake that she'd always regret. Even a seventeen-year-old makes mistakes that scare me!*

Cyndy sat up on the edge of her bed. *I have to talk to him again. I can't let him think I really do hate him. And I have to make him understand how I feel.*

Mr. Sanderson stood up. *I have to talk to her*, he thought. *I want her to know that I'm not mad at her and that I do trust her. I want her to know how much I love her and how much I worry about her when she's out there in the mean, ugly world.*

Cyndy walked to her door. With one hand on the doorknob, she stopped for a deep, calming breath. She opened the door and stood face to face with her dad, his hand raised ready to knock.

"I'm sorry," they both said at the same time. They both laughed and hugged each other.

It's not always easy to be part of a family. Anytime people live together, there's room for trouble. It's great to have people around who care about you. But sometimes, you wish that everyone related to you would disappear.

In some ways, it's harder to have a strong Christian family today than ever before. The typical family used to include a father who worked and a mother who stayed home. The families of today are quite different. In two-parent families, increasingly, both parents must work. In single-parent families, the one parent is usually the only one financially supporting the family.

This leaves kids on their own more than ever before. This trend in families is good news and bad news. The bad news is that sometimes kids are left without the support they need to make the best decisions. They are pressured to get involved in using alcohol, taking drugs, or in making decisions about sex at a time when the wrong choice can do more than emotional and spiritual damage; it can kill. Without the support of caring adults, some teens make choices they later regret.

The good news is that because teens are on their own more, they are learning to be

responsible earlier. To take charge of their own lives. Responsible teens are thinking through what their parents have taught them and are applying their Christianity to real life around them. It shows in their choices about entertainment, music, and lifestyle. They choose not to be involved in things that are harmful or lead them away from God.

Consider these ideas for getting along in your family:

1. **Make an effort to understand your parents, even when they drive you crazy!** Try to look past what they are doing, and find out why they are doing it.

2. **Be responsible.** Ask for the right to make decisions, but be responsible for the results. If you choose to stay up all night watching videos, don't expect your parents to cover for you or handle your work the next day.

3. **Treat your brothers or sisters like . . . people.** Show them a little respect. Give them a little space to be themselves. And if sometimes you just can't stand them, get away from them for a while.

4. **Settle your standards ahead of time.** Don't wait until you're in a difficult situation before deciding what you will do. Your best defense in a sticky situation is knowing "why not" before someone asks. Think about discussing things like drugs and sex with your parents. You might be surprised to learn how they dealt with these problems in their day.

5. **Do a family thing with God every week.** Help your family find the time for a special family worship. Maybe Friday night after supper or Sabbath afternoon would work. Maybe just sitting together in church would be good. Worshiping, singing, or just talking about God together will bring any family closer together.

It's good to know that God loves people with big problems, even when they are part of a family that has big problems. Some teenagers wonder if any family could be in worse shape than theirs. Well, the Bible tells a story of a family with big problems. Jacob's family.

Jacob's family is a good example of a "dysfunctional"

family. A dysfunctional family is one in which the relationships between the parents or between the parents and children aren't healthy. Sometimes the relationship is unhealthy because of abuse or neglect. Often the family members just don't know how to communicate with each other.

Jacob's family had several problems. God knew what was best when He planned that a man should have only one wife. Leah and Rachel may have been close as sisters, but the competition between them as wives was painful. Rachel was Jacob's favorite wife, and her sons were his favorites. And the other sons knew it. They became jealous and envious. They learned to hate Joseph.

Jacob created a lot of trouble for himself when he treated Joseph better than his brothers. Why would he do something that would cause so much trouble in the family? Maybe a brief review of his family's history will help in understanding Jacob as a parent.

He treated his children the same way he had been treated by his parents. Remember, his father Isaac had a favorite son. Isaac favored Esau. And Rebekah favored Jacob.

This favoritism caused many problems. The brothers argued, and they hated each other. Jacob's mother even worked out a plan to trick his father, Isaac, so that Jacob could have the birthright blessing. Esau got so mad he planned to kill Jacob, and Jacob had to run for his life.

And what about Isaac's family? His father, Abraham, yielded to Sarah's wishes and even sent his firstborn son, Ishmael, away permanently so that Isaac wouldn't have to share the inheritance.

The problems in Jacob's family were the result of bad parenting skills, poor communication, jealousy, and envy. Family problems like that are often passed on from one generation to the next. But it wasn't all bad. Jacob learned from his parents that he could trust God. And he passed that on to his children. He may have failed in many ways, but his sons knew that he had a real relationship with the true God.

If you think your family has serious problems that go deeper than just bad communication, consider these steps.

1. **Talk to an adult about it.**
   Just ignoring it until you

can leave home won't make it go away. Like Jacob, you could create similar problems in your own home.

2. If the problem is serious, get help yourself **so you can break the chain of family problems.**

3. If your family ties are weak, strengthen your ties to God. You'll need Him more than ever. Spend time talking and listening to Him every day.

God's plan for families is that they are to be the place where each person is loved and accepted with no strings attached. After all, He uses the concept of family to help us understand the kind of relationship He wants with humans. He wants us to be part of His family.

Memory Focus

"Children, obey your parents in the Lord, for this is right. 'Honor your father and mother'—which is the first commandment with a promise—'that it may go well with you and that you may enjoy long life on the earth.' Fathers, do not exasperate your children; instead, bring them up in the training and instruction of the Lord" (Ephesians 6:1-4, NIV).

Into the Bible

1. Genesis 37, portrays a number of attitudes that cause dissension and/or problems in a family. These are dishonesty, jealousy, rivalry, favoritism, anger, bitterness, envy, and pride. For each of the texts listed below, indicate the problem, the person responsible for the problem, and the result. Follow the example given.

   Verses 3, 4:
   Problem—favoritism

Person responsible—Jacob
Result—brothers hated Joseph
  A. Verses 5-8
  B. Verses 9-11
  C. Verse 18
  D. Verses 31-33
  E. Verses 34, 35

2. Genesis 37 records the terrible anger that Joseph's brothers had toward him and the results of their anger. Use a Bible concordance to find five texts on anger in the book of Proverbs and five texts on forgiveness in the book of Matthew. List the texts, and write the idea of each text. Then write a paragraph on how Christians should respond to those things that make them angry.

3. In spite of his success as the leader of his tribe, Jacob made many mistakes in his family life. Divide a sheet of paper into two columns. Use the headings SUCCESSES and FAILURES. Then list Jacob's successes and failures in his family life, as recorded in the following verses:

Genesis 25:27-34   Genesis 31:36-42
Genesis 27:22-34   Genesis 32:22-30
Genesis 28:10-22   Genesis 35:1-4, 9-15
Genesis 29:16-20   Genesis 37:2-4

 Projects

1. Sometimes it seems like Joseph could have saved himself a lot of trouble if he had kept his mouth shut. Every time he told about another of his dreams, his brothers hated him more. Read Genesis 37, and imagine that you lived in the tent next door. What advice would you give Joseph about getting along with his brothers?

2. Interview five other students. Ask these questions; then make up a report on their answers:

What one thing creates the most problems in your family?
What one thing do you enjoy the most?
What one thing would you change if you could?
What one thing could you do to make the family a happier place?

3. Like all children, Jacob learned much from his parents. Although he repeated some of the same mistakes, he was blessed by his parents' example. Make a list of five positive things you can learn from your parent(s) or guardian(s) that will help make you a happy Christian.

4. Families are affected by the positive and negative influences in our society. As you read magazines and newspapers or listen to the radio and watch TV, make a list of both the positive and negative influences on the family that you find. Share your findings with the class.

Focus Questions

1. Do you, like Cyndy in the story, ever say things that you wish you had never said? What do you do about it?
2. Do you think that allowing teens to make decisions for themselves will make them more responsible? Why or why not?
3. Who do you think was to blame for Joseph being sold as a slave? What percent of the blame goes to Jacob? To the older brothers? To Joseph?
4. What would be a good example of a dysfunctional family?
5. What should someone in a dysfunctional family do to help make the situation better?
6. Is it surprising that God chose Jacob's family as the beginning of His chosen people? What does that say about us and our families?

TRANSFORMATION

Let God transform you inwardly by a complete change of your mind
(Romans 12:2, Good News).

Joseph
PART I: FAITHFUL TO GOD AND FAMILY
Lesson Scripture: Genesis 37, 39-41

How about a new soft linen gown for the wedding?" Potiphar turned to face Ben Marduk, the Midianite merchant who provided balsam, incense, slaves, and silk to the Egyptian royal court. The craggy old merchant bowed low before the priest, his upstretched hands offering a flow of incredibly white linen, shot through with strands of pure gold.

"I've been saving it for you," Ben Marduk continued. "I knew when Asenath became a bride you would want the finest fabric available."

Potiphar caught his breath and knew instantly that he was going to make Ben Marduk a richer man. But that was all

right. He actually liked the old con artist, and Asenath would love the fabric.

"Ben Marduk, what do you know about my new son-in-law? I hear you brought him to Egypt tied to the back of a camel."

The merchant's laughter nearly drowned out the shouting and clanging of the bazaar.

"Three things I know, and three I will tell you. His brothers hated him because he was a spoiled son. You can thank his father for that! He's the smartest slave I've ever sold. You can probably thank his mother there. And the child became a man on my camel!"

"Became a man? How so?" Potiphar, priest of On, chief religious advisor to the great Pharaoh, caressed the shimmering fabric that Ben Marduk had laid enticingly in his hands.

"Ah! Let me tell you! Most everybody I know, children and old, become like scared sheep when in a really tight situation. Especially the spoiled ones. And this *wise* kid *Joseph*, wearing his father's multicolored long-sleeved prince's robe, was already a legend around the desert campfires.

"His brothers hated him so totally that he only cost me twenty silver pieces. But I wasn't sure I'd gotten a bargain. In fact, I worried that his attitude might make him a hard sale!"

Several of the brightly robed attendants in the priest's entourage moved closer, drawn by the crusty voice of a master story-teller.

"At first, all he did was wail, cry, scream, and threaten. But I just left him there, tied tight to old Shamgar's hump.

"But on the second night, he went dead silent. Kept looking off into the hills toward some nomad campfires. In the morning, he asked to see me. Called me in a soft, kind voice!

" 'Ben Marduk,' he said. 'Father taught me that when I'm in trouble I'd best be grown up and trust to Jehovah God. Those were Father's fires last night. He'll know I'm dead.

Gone. Done. I guess that means it's time to trust for real.'

"Potiphar, you should have seen him break into that magic smile. Right there, tied up on Shamgar. It was as if his whole life had been miraculously filled with glittering rainbows."

The morning sun created grand patterns on the merchant's face as he smiled confidentially at the priest.

"Then with his next words, Joseph taught this old merchant to smile. 'Since you'll be selling me in Egypt, could you teach me everything you know about the country, animals, merchants, and cloth? I'd like to be the best slave in all Egypt, and to do that I'm going to need your help.'"

"So you trained him for General Potiphar!" Potiphar was obviously impressed.

"Nope. Trained him to take over my caravan. General Potiphar only got him on a fluke. He made me an offer even I couldn't refuse!"

The attentions of both merchant and priest shifted back to the linen. They haggled down and up, finally settling on a fortune for both.

"That Joseph, your beautiful Asenath's new husband, he's got the finest mind I've ever met."

278

Ben Marduk slipped the gold into a leather pouch that hung safely under his embroidered cloak. Then he continued speaking.

"I think it's because he's chosen to belong to his God. Joseph's so loyal that he actually runs from anything his God doesn't OK! Just ask Mrs. Potiphar about that! Joseph's become as pure as that linen you are holding.

"Yes, sir. Your Asenath is one lucky woman. And you're one lucky priest. I'll bet even you'll learn a thing or two from the prime minister. I sure did.

"He taught me that choosing God grows you up, fills you with peace, and makes you into a trustworthy friend.

"A trustworthy friend and a linen gown. Your Asenath is greatly blessed!"

Interesting stuff you might like to know:

Potiphar was the chief priest in On (Hieropolis) and served as religious advisor to Pharaoh.

Roving merchants like Ben Marduk traveled Africa, Europe, and Asia trading anything they could purchase and resell. They served as supermarkets, drugstores, employment agencies, and clothing boutiques. They also served as the "network news." They knew everyone and everything, and everyone knew them.

Asenath, daughter of the priest Potiphar, was probably one of the most eligible women in all of Egypt, a perfect match for a trusted prime minister.

Jacob truly had spoiled Joseph, making him less than pleasant for everyone to live with. See Genesis 37:2-4.

Joseph's conversion occurred within sight of his home mountains. The main element in that conversion was a commitment to be loyal to God, *regardless!* See *Patriarchs and Prophets,* pages 213, 214.

True conversion changes the direction of life, allowing the power of Christ to transform selfish lives into ones that accurately represent Christ. See Colossians 3:1-17.

The Bible gives five major illustrations of Joseph's faithfulness and loyalty:

1. His faithfulness to Potiphar as his chief servant.
2. His faithfulness to God in Potiphar's bedroom.
3. His faithfulness to the jailer.
4. His faithfulness to his father and family.
5. His faithfulness to Pharaoh as his prime minister. ⚱

 **Memory Focus**

"Whatever you do, whether in word or deed, do it all in the name of the Lord Jesus, giving thanks to God the Father through him" (Colossians 3:17, NIV).

 **Into the Bible**

1. Envy or jealousy was a problem in Joseph's Canaan home. Consider God's solutions for envious attitudes, and then suggest three things Joseph could have done to reduce the jealous tension in his home. Use the following texts to begin your study.

   A. Galatians 5:19-24
   B. James 3:13-18
   C. 1 Corinthians 13:4
   D. 1 Corinthians 3:3-9

2. Loyalty was one of Joseph's strongest traits of character. Read the following Bible passages, and then write a "Code of Christian Loyalty" with which God empowers His children.

   A. Titus 2:14   F. Nehemiah 5:12, 13
   B. 1 Peter 2:13, 14   G. Philippians 2:3
   C. 1 Peter 2:15, 16   H. Philippians 2:13
   D. Romans 13:8   I. Matthew 5:9
   E. Ecclesiastes 12:13, 14

3. Choose one of the following stories of conversion and commitment. Read the Bible passages, and then write a summary of what you have learned about conversion, commitment, and God's support of His children.

   • The Philippian jailer: Acts 16:24-33.
   • The Gadarene demoniac: Mark 5.
   • Saul/Paul: Acts 9:1-12; 21:13.

 # Projects

1. Write out the commitment prayer Joseph might have prayed from the hump of Ben Marduk's camel. Then write out a similar conversion prayer, one that you could pray to effectively bring the transforming power of God into your life. Be specific about what you would like for God to do in you.
2. Joseph's commitment did not necessarily mean that he would become and stay a faithful and loyal person. List five things Joseph could have done to maintain his conversion commitment. Star the ones that would also be the most beneficial to you.
3. Assume that Joseph lives in your community. What everyday activities around you could seriously erode his conversion commitment?

 # Focus Questions

1. What could have happened to Joseph if he hadn't made the conversion commitment? Is there anything happening in your life right now that could be improved by making a conversion commitment?
2. Often Satan twists us into very uncomfortable situations, tight places where we respond almost automatically with anger, self-centeredness, and frustration. Yet each of these responses is destructive. God challenges us that the only wise solution is to back away and turn the situation over to Him. Using Joseph's commitment as a guide, what can you do that can assist you in meeting any challenges you may meet?

PART II: JOSEPH AND HIS BROTHERS
Lesson Scripture: Genesis 42-45

 am Hiro, a free man and chief steward of the governor of Egypt. Although my eyes and ears have seen and heard many wonders during my duties, none compares with the coming of my master's brothers.

I do not speak easily of personal matters, but you have asked, and I will tell you what I have seen and heard.

The governor is a great man, always fair and eager to meet the needs of each who comes to him for assistance. He is also a great friend to me and the other servants. It is almost as if he sees in us the family he lost so long ago.

I first met part of the lost family during the second year of the great drought. The Nile guards brought news of a small donkey caravan coming from the northern desert mountains. "A group of dusty strangers," they said.

The governor ordered us to watch them closely and bring them to the official reception hall. The strangers from Canaan followed us with obvious fear.

The governor took them to be spies, became greatly upset about their visit, and grilled them about family, homes, brothers, crops, and herds. They answered well, but with great awe from their bowed positions at his feet. They reminded me of sheaves of grain doing obeisance before him.

"Take all ten men to Old Tisroc in the dungeon," the governor commanded me. Then he whispered, "They are to talk to no one except Tisroc. Tell him these are the ones for whom we have waited."

Three days later, I brought ten very humble and silent men back for another interview with the governor. He was direct, once again. "You are probably spies, but because I believe in God, I am going to let you go home anyway. However, to prove your story, I am demanding that you bring your other brother with you when you return for more grain. And to make sure you do as I order, I am keeping one of you in prison."

They gasped, argued among themselves in their odd-sounding language, and finally grew silent. The governor pointed out a middle-aged bearded one. "That one," the governor ordered, "keep him as a guarantee of their return."

One of the guards led the one they called Simeon off to Tisroc's dungeon.

Then the dusty, bearded strangers left, practically racing their donkeys to get away from the confusing events of their four days in Egypt.

I watched, knowing why Simeon had been selected for the dungeon and knowing that their confusion was only beginning.

To eat, and to retrieve Simeon, they would have to return. To see the governor again, they would have to bring young Benjamin. Then, when they brought Benjamin, we would know if they had forgiven themselves for the angry and hateful actions they had done to others. We would know if they had changed.

Joseph had shared the truth about his past with only a few of his trusted aides. Two of us, Tisroc and I, were crucial to the test he was giving his family. Long ago, he had forgiven them

for what they had done to him. Now he was determined to see if they had learned to trust God enough to make them safe citizens of Egypt.

We took good care of Simeon and watched for the return of the "nine-plus-one."

They came, weeks after we expected them, their sacks bulging with the best their country had to offer. And there were ten of them.

Soldiers led them to the residence of the governor. "The governor welcomes you to Egypt and invites you to a feast in honor of your return," I told them through an interpreter. "Please wash and be at your places before noon."

While they unloaded the donkeys, I listened and watched. These were the men who had thrown the governor into a pit and proclaimed him dead. These were the very men whose ugly hatred had led them to "murder."

Joseph should kill them immediately, I thought. *They deserve long, slow, and painful deaths. Instead, he is inviting them to dinner.*

I sat them in the prescribed order, oldest to youngest, on the other side of the brightly tiled room from the governor's table.

When he arrived, they

gushingly showered him with balsam, honey, pistachios, and more. Everything but the "key to Canaan." I ordered the food served. The servants brought the meal to them, oldest first and youngest last, with Benjamin receiving five times the portion of the others. This was the big test. They had hated Rachel's older son. Did they hate the younger also? Or were they different men, touched by the power of their God?

The governor watched and listened, hoping he was eating with honest, forgiven men.

Amazingly, none showed the hostility, envy, and ugliness I had expected. *Maybe*, I thought, *Joseph's forgiveness is being rewarded. Maybe it is safe for these men to become citizens of Egypt.*

I quickly made preparations for the last test. The brothers left the granary with heavily laden donkeys, believing they had grain. I knew they had grain, money, *and a cup.* Joseph's treasured antique cup had been placed, at his command, into Benjamin's sack.

He let them travel far out of sight and then motioned for me to do my duty. The guards rode before me, making an impressive flash of crimson and gold across the red desert.

"Halt! Halt! I command you to halt!" My shouts brought their happy trip to a terrified standstill. "You have taken the governor's personal cup. It is one of the treasures of Egypt, and you have stolen it from us all! Is this how you repay kindness?"

With a wave to the guards, I commanded them to begin their search. "Whoever has done this vile thing will become the governor's lowest slave."

I watched each face intently as I shouted, for their response would show all the governor wanted to know.

The answer was as clear as the reflection of my helmet in the silver cup. Around me, nine men wept for their own sins. None accused Benjamin of being the "guilty brother." Instead, each offered his own life in exchange for that of Benjamin. These were no longer the same men who had brought the bloody long-sleeved cloak to their father.

"Bring them to the reception hall," I commanded. Then I rode ahead to give Joseph the good news.

His forgiveness had been rewarded with faithfulness. His family could come home. ⊀

Memory Focus

"God sent me ahead of you to preserve for you a remnant on earth and to save your lives by a great deliverance" (Genesis 45:7, NIV).

. . . .

Into the Bible

1. Read Genesis 42:21, 22. Are the brothers truly sorry at this point?
2. Why did Joseph react the way he did in Genesis 42:24?
3. What is Benjamin's role in the family (Genesis 42:36-38)?
4. Reuben failed, in Genesis 42:37, 38, to convince Israel to let them take Benjamin to Egypt. How does Judah convince Israel to let them take Benjamin along? Read Genesis 43:3-10. Why does Judah succeed where Reuben failed?
5. What was Joseph's steward's response to the brothers' story about the silver in the sacks (Genesis 43:19-23)?
6. Why do you think Joseph had the brothers sit in the order of their ages at the table (Genesis 43:32-34)?
7. Why do you think Joseph placed the silver cup in Benjamin's sack (Genesis 44:1, 2)?
8. Do the brothers seem willing to take the blame for their wrong actions (Genesis 44:6-10)? Is this the same attitude, or a different one from Genesis 37:12-36?
9. Read Genesis 44:15. Is Joseph lying here?
10. Would you say that the brothers' response to getting caught with the cup in Genesis 44:16 was a mature response to being found out? Why?
11. God has the ability to make good come out of bad situations. Examine Romans 8:28. How could Paul have used this story to illustrate what he says in Romans 8:28?

 **Project**

Joseph revealed himself to his brothers in a most unusual manner. Complete the Personal Feelings chart provided by your teacher. Compare your answers with others in the class, and then discuss together how one decides whether or not to reveal something very personal to another person.

. . . .

 Focus Questions

1. What parallels can you think of between the relationship of Joseph and his brothers and Christ's relationship with us?
2. Why is forgiveness such an important power in relationships? What would relationships be like if forgiveness were not a possibility?
3. When someone has deeply wronged you, are you more likely to seek revenge or reconciliation? Be honest. Can you think of an illustration of each in your life?
4. What principles learned from Joseph's life would apply to us today?

PART III: MRS. POTIPHAR'S INVITATION
Lesson Scripture: Genesis 39

She was a beautiful friend. And I was but the slave of her husband. The *trusted* slave of her husband.

I had become a slave one lonely Egyptian morning when Ben Marduk, the "quality-goods" Midianite trader, sold me to General Potiphar. The heat was intense, the guards pushy, and the other slaves sullen.

"Watch out for the big soldier," the tall slave next to me whispered. "They say he loves to beat his slaves. Make sure you don't get sold to Potiphar."

I shuffled, slumped, looked foolish, and tried my best to be "poor quality," but Potiphar was too sharp for my acting.

"Who is the boy, Marduk?" The general's voice sounded harshly cruel. "I need a young man with a mind. Does his still work?"

I listened as they haggled over my price, the trader always protesting that he was being robbed by the general's large offers. The slave beside me poked and whispered again, "Your father could have purchased a herd of camels with that gold. You'd better be worth it!"

I decided to show them all that the general had made a good investment. As I put on the robe of Potiphar's slaves, I also decided to stay true to my commitment as Jehovah's friend. Even in the general's house.

Potiphar's slaves were industrious and wise. I befriended them, asked questions, listened to their answers, and worked hard at the mundane tasks assigned me.

And all of the time I felt her eyes. She was watching me walk, watching me work. At first, she would quickly glance away when I looked up and caught her gaze. But as the months passed, and as my duties took me more often into the house, her look became bold and playful.

The general assigned me to rough shepherding in the hills. I liked the animals and loved being in the freedom of outdoors. I easily made friends with the other shepherds and made suggestions that improved the health of the animals and the ease of caring for them. Father's herds had taught me well.

Then Potiphar shifted my responsibilities from the mundane to the complex.

"You are to be overseer of the shepherds and herdsmen." Potiphar's voice didn't sound nearly as cruel as the day he had bought me. "You're intelligent. Make sure all of the herds grow fat!"

Less than a year later, he was back with a new challenge. "Joseph, Zadok died last night. I need a chief steward to take his place, and you're the man!" I wanted to collapse in shock. Instead, I straightened my back and listened to Potiphar describe the task. "Everything I own is now yours to care for. The houses, the lands, the animals, the barns. Even the other slaves. I'm giving you responsibility for everything except my food and my wife."

We talked often after that, and with each conversation our friendship deepened. I basked in the glow of being trusted by the master, who had become my friend.

We traveled together in the fields and surveyed my new irrigation systems. High on the peaks, we tested the rich wool that was thickening on our sheep. Near the river, we walked together through the rooms of the new home that had been designed to match the beauty and desires of a general's wife.

Always he asked my advice and trusted my answers. While he left no doubt that all of this belonged to him, he smiled with pleasure as I treated it as if it were my own.

I was trusted! And I reveled in the joy of acceptance. Acceptance and trust from both my God and my master.

The work was the most difficult when the general was away. Then, with other key servants and slaves, I guided the planting, harvesting, shearing, repairing, and other events of Egyptian life.

And always she watched.

"Please, Joseph." Her eyelashes fluttered the requests. "May I go with you to see the lambs? I love traveling in the fields. Please?" I took her along to the fields, mountains, canals, river, and to the house the general had designed for the lady who waited for her warrior to return.

I grew more and more

uncomfortable with my feelings.

I have felt eyes like hers before. Leah often had them for my father. All the Canaanite girls fluttered their lashes at Judah and Simeon. And the market prostitutes flash hot smiles at every man who passes by.

But her looks sizzled with a greater fire. They burned right through my clothes, leaving me feeling naked and vulnerable before her.

I stayed away, or at least made certain I walked with several other servants. I focused my thoughts away from everything sexual. I kept my eyes off her face and body.

But she was beautiful, with a beauty that called to me in a voice that was difficult to ignore. Around her, it was hard to remember why I loved Jehovah.

And she was always there. Smiling, asking questions, reaching out to touch my hand, inviting me to join her on private trips to "check the doors" in the new Nile home.

"No, I'm busy with the shepherds." "No, but I will send young Ahmed with you." "No, I'm sorry." I tried all of the excuses I could form, but she continued asking, inviting, and dressing to entice.

Father's words haunted me. "The enemy will try to trip you. But Jehovah will provide an escape for every temptation. Your challenge is to choose the escapes rather than the temptations."

Hot and heady, that challenge found me one morning at the Nile.

I felt her eyes caressing me as I worked near the entrance to her rooms. The baths of milk and honey had softened her skin and deepened it to a glowing gold, a glow that now filled my eyes and urged my arms to gather it in. Her open arms offered even more. And urged it.

Every muscle in my body moved her way in consent. Every cell of my mind commanded me to flee.

Then a voice exploded into my senses with His offer of escape. "You cannot answer the enemy's call and remain true to your master Potiphar and to your Lord Jehovah.

"And they trust you!"

Interesting stuff you might like to know:

Adultery was unacceptable behavior in Egyptian society, just as it was for the Hebrews. In

fact, sexual activity outside of marriage is prohibited in most cultures of the world.

If Potiphar had believed his wife's report of Joseph's attempted rape, Joseph would have been quickly sentenced to death. The fact that Joseph ended up in prison, alive, indicates that the general understood both his wife and his chief steward. The prison was located "in Potiphar's house." See Genesis 40:3.

Memory Focus

"No temptation has seized you except what is common to man. And God is faithful; he will not let you be tempted beyond what you can bear. But when you are tempted, he will also provide a way out so that you can stand up under it" (1 Corinthians 10:13, NIV).

Into the Bible

1. Read David's song of repentance (Psalm 51). Describe the effects of confession, repentance, and forgiveness upon the scars of sin.
2. Do a thematic study of purity and chastity, using the following texts. Describe how God's attitude toward these virtues affects the lives of Christian teenagers today.

   Purity: Psalm 24:3, 4; Matthew 5:8; 1 Timothy 1:5; 1 Timothy 5:22; 1 Peter 1:22.
   Chastity: Deuteronomy 5:18; Job 31:1; Proverbs 5:20; Matthew 5:28; 1 Thessalonians 4:3, 4; Titus 2:4-8.
3. Contrast the stories of Joseph and Samson (Genesis 39 and Judges 16). What gave Joseph the strength to remain pure? What moved Samson to choose immorality?

4. Read Genesis 45:1-24. Verses in this chapter contain phrases that describe words or acts from Joseph's experience that correlate with Jesus' life. On the worksheet provided by your teacher, state an act or the words from Joseph's experience that show him to be a type of Christ.

 # Project

Visit the magazine rack at your local market or library.

A. Examine five of the magazines, and write down the titles of the stories listed on the covers. Also note the photographs on the covers.
B. Indicate which stories look interesting enough to read.
C. Indicate which of the stories and photos would help you develop stronger Christian sexual values.
D. What guidelines do you use in selecting what you read or think about?

 # Focus Questions

Four more questions to help you personalize the faithfulness of Joseph's life:

1. What impact did Joseph's commitment to God have on his success as Potiphar's servant?
2. What could have been the result if Joseph had given in to Mrs. Potiphar's request?
3. What kept Joseph faithful? He was far from home, with no friends, and no church members watching. What value was there in staying faithful?
4. Why was Joseph concerned about "sinning against God"? Why not just accept her offer for sex?

ACKNOWLEDGMENTS

Grateful acknowledgment and recognition is given to those who made a valuable contribution to the development of books 1 and 2 of the **CROSSROADS SERIES** for grades 9 and 10—**IN THE BEGINNING GOD . . . and GOD'S GIFT ♦ OUR CHOICE**.

• SECONDARY BIBLE TEXTBOOK STEERING COMMITTEE •

The following served on the Secondary Bible Textbook Steering Committee and were responsible for supervising development of Student Textbooks, Teacher's Edition, and Teacher Resource Manual for **IN THE BEGINNING GOD . . . and GOD'S GIFT ♦ OUR CHOICE**.

Gerry E. Thompson, chair
Ed Boyatt
Richard Fredericks
Gordon Kainer
Edward M. Norton
Glenn E. Russell
Don L. Weatherall

• CONSULTANTS AND STAFF •

The following provided valuable support services to the Steering Committee during the development of one or more components.

Bonnie Casey, editorial assistance.

Victor H. Fullerton, coordinator.

Shirley Goodridge, editorial assistant and copyright authorizations.

Marion Hartlein, North American Division Office of Education consultant.

Alyce Pudewell, art consultant.

Lorene Beaulieu, word processing and formatting of manuscripts for Student Textbook and Teacher's Edition.

Beverly Benson, word processing of manuscripts for Student Textbook and Teacher's Edition.

Ardyce Weatherall, word processing of manuscripts for Teacher's Edition and Teacher Resource Manual.

• WRITERS •

The following functioned as writers of one or more lessons. Each writer brought to his or her work a rich background of experiences and a writing style that adds interest and variety in approaches to the topics covered.

DeWayne Boyer, Greg Brothers, Steve Case, Renee Coffee, Des Cummings, Jr., Richard Duerksen, Richard Fredericks, L. R. Holmes, Gordon Kainer, Gayle Norton, Jerry Thomas, Alden Thompson, Stuart Tyner, Martin Weber.

• TEACHERS AND STUDENTS •

The 67 teachers and approximately 1500 students in junior and senior academies of the North American Division who field tested lessons during the 1993-1994 school year. Their responses on the survey questionnaires provided valuable input and insights.

• TEACHER RESOURCE MANUAL WORKSHOP COMMITTEE •

The following Bible teachers and other education personnel served on the 1994 summer workshop committee that developed the Teacher Resource Manual.

Don L. Weatherall, Chair
Ron Aguilera
Lyle Bennett
Brett Hadley
Gordon Kainer
Victor H. Fullerton
Gerry E. Thompson

• PACIFIC PRESS PUBLISHING ASSOCIATION •

Paul A. Hey, liaison with the Secondary Bible Textbook Steering Committee

Robert Mason and Michelle C. Petz, designers

Glen Robinson, editor

• PUBLISHERS, AUTHORS, AND AGENTS •

Grateful acknowledgment is made to the following publishers, authors, and agents for permission to use and adapt copyrighted materials.

Opening Quotations for lessons are from the following sources: The Bible - Good News (30); New International Version (4, 15); The Living Bible (3, 11); *The Daily Walk* devotional pamphlets (2, 6, 12, 17, 29); Gordon Kainer (13, 19, 27); C. S. Lewis (23); *14,000 Quips and Quotes* (1, 7, 8, 9, 10, 14, 16, 18, 20, 22, 24, 26); Unknown (5, 21); Mary Shelley (28); Ellen G. White, *Counsels to Teachers*, p. 53 (25).

Illustrations for opening pages of units and lessons were provided by the following: pp. 8-9, Mark Lewis/Picturesque Inc.; p. 12, Daniel J. Cox/Tony Stone Images; p. 18, Harvey Lloyd/The Stock Market; p. 26, David Lawrence/The Stock Market; p. 36, Peter Brandt; p. 46, Jose Fuste Raga/The Stock Market; p. 58, John W. Warden/Superstock; p. 72, Jaime Villaseca/The Image Bank; pp.

80-81, Chris Noble/Tony Stone Images; p. 84, FPG International; p. 92, Joel Rogers/Tony Stone Images; p. 104, D. Maitland/FPG International; p. 114, Kenneth Eward; p. 122, James R. Amos/Superstock; p. 130, FPG International; p. 136, Chris Collins/The Stock Market; p. 144, Clark Mishler/Alaska Stock Images; pp. 152-153, Art Wolfe/Tony Stone Images; p. 156, Charles Blecker; p. 164, Martin Fox/Picturesque Inc.; p. 170, Chris Noble/Tony Stone Images; p. 178, Ken Cooper/The Image Bank; p. 186, Charles Blecker; p. 194, Gary Jensen/Picturesque, Inc.; p. 200, Johny Johnson/Tony Stone Images; pp. 208-209, Superstock; p. 212, Jeff Hunter/The Image Bank; p. 222, Bert Sagara/Tony Stone Images; p. 232, The Image Bank; p. 240, Michael DeYoung/Alaska Stock Images; p. 248, John Terence Turner/FPG International; p. 258, Art Wolfe/Tony Stone Images; p. 268, Randi Wells/Tony Stone Images; p. 276, Myron J. Dorf/The Stock Market.

Cover illustration by FPG International.

All Scripture references not otherwise credited are from the *Holy Bible: New International Version.*

Every effort has been made to trace the ownership of all copyrighted material in this book and to obtain permission for its use.
Sincere appreciation is given to the many others who have contributed to the manuscript whose names may not be included.

Thanks